The Evening Sun
Growing Old Beautifully

The Evening Sun
Growing Old Beautifully

By Joseph Folliet
(Brother Juniper)

translated by
David Smith

Franciscan Herald Press
1434 W. 51st St.
Chicago, IL 60609

The Evening Sun, Growing Old Beautifully by Joseph Folliet, translated by David Smith from the French *Le Soleil du Soir,* Paris: Editions du Centurion. American edition published with original publisher's permission.

Library of Congress Cataloging in Publication Data

Folliet, Joseph.
The evening sun.

Translation of: Le soleil du soir.
1. Old age. I. Title.
HQ1061.F5813 305.2′6 81-9780
ISBN 0-8199-0817-7 AACR2

MADE IN THE UNITED STATES OF AMERICA

To those excellent old men
who were my friends
and are now my models—
Louis Cousin
Marianist
Henri Colas
singer
Ernest Lancelot
companion of Saint Francis
Colonel André Roullet
and Joseph Vialatoux
of the *Chronique Sociale*

Contents

The Evening Sun

I have always loved the evening sun. This may be because I sleep so well in the morning that I find it a great effort to wake up and go, like Jeannot Lapin, to "woo the dawn." What is certain is that it is because the sunsets where I was brought up in the Rhône Valley are slow to reach maturity in the summer and autumn and even slower to die and they are so beautiful that they dazzle your heart.

The light of those sunsets persists in the depths of my being. They vividly recall my childhood and youth. And so many colors! Those sharp light greens at dusk! Those flaming scarlets! Those purples that glow like wine—the wine of Burgundy. Those yellows that remind me of the fields of yellow-flowered rape and those washed out and pale blues that so soon take on the brilliance of red and then the deep calm of the dark indigo of night! What a spectrum, a disordered and constantly moving rainbow! What a firework display above the tops of the poplar trees. In my memory, I wait for the last gleams that tinge the willows with purple and then skim over the earth like a sickle blade.

In the tropics, the evening sun is a ball of fire that disappears so quickly into the sea that you can almost hear it hissing. In Italy, the setting sun stretches a red and gold curtain across the sky like a great tent. In the countryside around Lyon and in the great valley where I spent my youth, however, the damp air rising from the Rhône spreads and extends the clear light of the evening sun and transforms it into a living being that seems to want to delay its departure and enjoy itself for a while, sorry that it has to leave the men whose footsteps and work it has guided throughout the day. It consents to die, but only a very easy death, after a solemn and dignified agony. The dawns in that part of the world are silver and crystal; the sunsets are melted gold and precious stones.

And as it is spreading the light of the departing sun, the evening is also radiating peace. The heavy heat of the day is followed by a light wind that descends from the mountains and gently shakes the leaves of the aspens. The same breeze bends the columns of smoke from the chimneys of the houses to which workers and flocks are returning and where the last meal of the day is almost ready. On it is carried by the tinkling of the Angelus bell. It bears aloft the bats which are leaving their haunts as they always do at twilight to make their first flight of the night. The peace of evening is the prelude to the quiet rest of the night.

I loved them very much, those evening hours when the rays of the declining sun mingled with those of the first star. Sitting at my window of our house on the hill of the Croix-Rousse to the northwest of Lyon, I could see the last fires of the day outlining the hills of the Mont d'Or region with bright red. Or, going back to the Croix-Rousse after wandering round all day in the countryside, I often paused to listen to the last song of the birds in the bushes nestling in the sunken paths. How sorry I am for those who have lived entirely in towns and have never known, when they were young, what I knew as a boy or who spent days in the country, but perhaps never learned to listen and look as I did.

* * *

The evening sun and my first glimpses of old age are for ever linked together in my memories. I can still see them—the old folk sitting outside their houses at dusk eating their soup. They ate it by soaking their bread in it, the one flavoring the other, and that alone was their evening meal. While they ate, they would chat discreetly with their neighbors on the other side of the street.

They were the last people to do this. The younger members of their families were already more middle class in their attitudes and ate inside their houses. What did the old people want from this half-hour each evening? They wanted, food, relaxation, and friendly contact with each other. I was a town boy, but, released for a few weeks from the constraints of town manners and free to enjoy nature, I used to imitate my grandparents. I sat on the stone doorstep or at the foot of the stairs near the door and dipped my spoon in a bowl of soup smelling and tasting of cabbage, beans, and other vegetables.

In this way, I learned how to distinguish between ages and especially how to situate old age. For me, old age will always be old men in clogs and old women in white bonnets eating their soup on their doorsteps in the evening sun. Rightly or wrongly, I think that this picture of old people is better than that of old middle-class ladies in their drawing rooms smelling of camphor or poor little old men in their homes for the aged with a little less space to live in than a twelve-year-old schoolboy and hardly a little more freedom.

* * *

Old age and evening have often been compared with each other. Old age as the evening of life is a commonplace cliché, of course, but the comparison is still valid. Like evening, old age is an end—the end of the day, the conclusion of a pilgrimage. Like evening, it points to the melancholy of everything that has to come to an end, the sadness of what is fragile. Like evening too, which is an invitation to night, old age is an introduction to death.

But what is forgotten so easily is that the evening of life can also be the evening sun and that it contains both a promise and a consolation. We forget that the evening sun can be just as beautiful as the sun that shines in the early morning or at midday and sometimes even more beautiful. It not only bathes our tired eyes in its gentle light and warms our old ears—it also assures us that the light and the heat do not die. It will be day again tomorrow. We may have to go through the night, it is true, but we shall come to the end of it and our journey to the end of night is never desperate wandering. At the end of the night, a new sun is shining.

The old folk of my youth were very wise to enjoy the setting sun as they did. They found in it both a compensation and a hope. The old people of today, living in the artificial light and heat of the cities, think too readily of the sadness of the evening and of the night that inexorably follows. It is for them that I have written this book.

* * *

Yes, I am writing for you, my brothers and sisters of my own age, in the cold shadow of night. But I am also writing for myself. I too have just crossed the frontier from which no one can return. I would like us to contemplate together the evening sun and together to be aware of the joys that it holds in store for us. They are, we know, our last joys, but they are still joys and, even more, they are a foretaste of the joys that we shall taste in God's eternity.

I know that it is not sunny every day. There are misty, rainy, cold, and even stormy days. But we should never let go of those evenings when the sun sends us its wealth and splendor. We should never let them slip by because we are indifferent or full of resentment or bad humor. We should open our eyes and our hearts—keep them wide open to the evening light. We should gather it into our innermost being and treasure it for the gloomy days. Let us, then, go forward from light to light toward the ultimate brilliance that will shine between time and eternity.

But I am writing for you too—young men and girls, mature men and women and indeed all of you, to help you to understand that old age is not a gradual extinction, but something much richer. The Lord, who is the master of our life, gives old people the grace of many evening suns. So you younger people should be able to show something other than scorn or the pity that is so near to scorn to old age. The sun at dawn, the midday sun and the evening sun—it is always the same sun! And the sun of time that changes with the hour of the day and the season of the year bears the image of the sun of eternity.

The Winter Sun

I have called to mind the summer and autumn suns, but there are also the winter suns and these are no less beautiful and certainly no less precious. We can see the rays of the winter sun in the paintings of Breughel and sense them in the music of Vivaldi.

The comparison between old age and winter is older than literature and takes us into the realm of folklore. The winter is the last season of the year. It is the end of a cycle. The days are short and the nights are long. Men and women withdraw into themselves and live cosily in the artificial heat of their homes and in the fields the earth resists all attempts to work it, in the hard grip of frost or the softness of the snow. Winter is also the time of illness—colds and coughs, running noses, and rheumatism stiffening the arms and legs.

Winter and all that accompanies it reminds us of old age—the time of life when we are condemned to idleness and great care, when our muscles are made rigid and our blood and sometimes even our hearts are colder and when our minds cloud over. Old age—the winter of life—is the last stage and the prelude to what is often called the last end. Images come to mind—a little old man muffled up and going for his walk and

Villon's old women squatting down in front of their meager fire of brushwood, what we call a widow's fire in the Rhône Valley.

I think it is a good comparison, old age and winter, so long as it is not taken too far, since, thank God, winter is neither so simple nor so sad. I loved winter when I was young, especially sliding and snowball fights, and I still love it.

I love the biting north wind of winter that freezes the end of your nose and the tips of your ears, but at the same time wakes you up and makes you vigorous and young again. I love the white expanses of snow that make fertile nature a virgin again. I love the frost that makes the earth like metal and rings under your steps.

Above all I love the winter suns. Sometimes the sun is seen in winter at the end of a misty morning like a huge ball of frozen flame and sometimes I have seen it spreading its rays over the snow and making a hundred thousand sparks crackle. I can remember traveling by sleigh in Canada, one half of my body in the shadow and frozen and the other half in the sun and burning! I can also recall the fire of the setting sun in the depths of winter lightly touching the crystals of snow and painting it with so many unexpected colors. Their cold and biting acid were to the eye what the sharp taste of the gooseberry is to the mouth.

I want old age to be like winter, because the traditional comparison invites me to think of it in this way. But I do not think of that winter of old age as cold and grey. It is full of light—a light which is more friendly because it is rare and fleeting and well worth the trouble to gather as a source of joy.

"May sun, sun of my youth" was a popular song at the beginning of the century in France, but why should we not sing another song now: "Winter sun, sun of my old age?" The winter sun is paler than the sun of my youth, but it recalls the sun of those days and does so with a gentleness tinged with a trace of melancholy. It is a sun that warms my old blood and gives life to my old heart. It is a sun that revives me because it tells me that the winter will not last forever and that the resurrection of spring will come again in the glory of Easter.

Two Sunny Portraits

Some old people have faces which reflect the setting sun's rays and the finest days of winter. When we want to describe the springtime of life, we speak of the green years, but we know too that old age can also be green. A trace of spring remains in old age and even until death. The two faces that I want to present in this chapter were like that and love has engraved their features on my memory. I have taken both of them from my family album.

* * *

My grandmother on my mother's side, Claudine Labeye, was one of those classical old ladies whom one could meet then, as Baudelaire has said: In the winding folds of the old capital cities.

She always wore a black dress with a very long wide skirt, so full of pockets that she never needed to carry a handbag, a black bonnet with a great deal of lace and a few jade ornaments and big shoes into which her arthritic feet fitted easily. She claimed that she had gone on growing until she was thirty, but she had in fact remained tiny—a little object made of yellowed ivory. Her face was rather masculine and she had a long, sharp nose—no fine bell tower had ever spoilt the beauty of her village, she used to say—and this gave her an affinity, when she was serious, with the Curé d'Ars and, when she was malicious, with Voltaire. She left the village in Savoy where she was born when she was fourteen, worked in a silk spinning mill, married my grandfather, a metal worker, rather late in life and had three children—two boys and a girl. She had experienced all the hardships of working-class life of that period.

But even at the happiest moments of her life she was always hard up. Yet she did everything so well that, when she was in her fifties and so ill that all the doctors said she would not live to see sixty, she lived on to bury them all and stubbornly last out until she was ninety-four. Those people from Savoy in the nineteenth century—they were tough and clung to life like the wiry bushes growing on the sides of their limestone cliffs.

After her husband had died, her children looked after her so well that she had a secure and calm old age. She made the most of it! As long as her health was good and her mind was active, she walked two or three miles a day to a bench on the Croix-Rousse to have a chat with her contemporaries. In the park around the Gros Caillou, that great erratic block left here by the glaciers that shaped the land on which Lyon was built, they would talk interminably and, in clear weather, look over the city eastwards, across the great plain of the Bas-Dauphiné to the Alps. They would go on talking until the setting sun told them that they had to go home.

She was a good Christian. Her faith was built of lime and sand on the rock that formed its base and she had brought it from her native village. But she was not perfect. She had a sharp tongue. But how can her grandson, who has sinned so much with his own tongue and with his pen, reproach her for that? After all, she was very amusing—precisely because of this imperfection. She remained gay and lively until the very end. Of course, she talked too much, but almost everything she said was funny, and she had an immense fund of racy stories. Sometimes she would hum the songs of her younger days and sometimes even sing them. Her voice was broken, but still true and she sang at times dramatically and at others maliciously. She often repeated herself, of course, but in spite of everything she continued to entertain me greatly.

I know now almost exactly how much I owe to her—a repertory of anecdotes that are still funny, a taste for folklore and a sense of the past. In a word—roots.

She died almost without noticing it, although she was quite proud of her great age. "She's only a girl," she said of one of her cronies, "She is only eighty." She passed from time into eternity quite gently, as though she was falling asleep.

* * *

My great-uncle, Gabriel Folliet, did not live as long as my grandmother from Savoy, but long enough to become acquainted with old age. He stayed firmly rooted in the village from which our family had come, where he plied his trade all his life. He was a cobbler or, as they came later to be called, a shoe repairer. This humble trade enabled him to be independent, and independence is something that all the Folliets have always greatly valued. It also made it possible for him to practice good relationships with other people and, to judge from the number of visits that he received, they must have been good. In order to be quite free and dependent on no one, he had saved enough to buy a piece of land and to have a little house built there. It made me think of an old log cabin.

A robust, healthy little old man, with thick straight hair that stayed black to the end of his days, a round nose covered with a network of fine red streaks and eyes that were round, black and glowing like large black currants.

There had been heights and depths in his life. The heights had not been very high, but the depths had often been quite deep. He had known misery, and he knew what it was to have too little to live on. He had been engaged for seven years before he had enough to marry on—seven years, like Jacob waiting for Laban! But these difficulties had never changed him for the worst. He remained good humored, despite many injustices, and bore no one ill-will. He was, I think, physically incapable of hatred and bitterness. His experience of life had reinforced his strong sense of social justice.

He was undoubtedly wise, cultured, and thoughtful, like so many shoe repairers of the period, but it was a peasant wisdom which made him retain a sense of the earth, an understanding of nature, animals, and plants and an insight into human experience which benefited me greatly as a young man. When his customers brought their footwear to him to be resoled or heeled, they consulted him about all kinds of things—their own personal difficulties, family troubles, matters to do with work and local or national politics. He always listened patiently even to chattering or boring people and he listened attentively. Then, taking the nails out of his mouth, he would speak calmly and deliberately, but never impose his will. He always avoided discussions that might have made him lose patience with other people.

Young people loved him. They often came to spend the evening with him. He was, in a sense, everybody's uncle. With him in the evening, there was a little drinking and a great deal of talking. There was even singing. It was at Uncle Gabriel's that I first learned how to sing and to tell stories. Young couples used to confide in Gabriel and tell him of their hopes and their disappointments.

His political views and the mistakes made by local priests had made him set a distance between himself and—not Christianity, for he had faith and Christian love in his blood—but from the Church. Toward the end of his life, when he began to see things from a higher level, he saw further than the ambiguities and misunderstandings and became one of the few men in the district to go regularly to Sunday Mass.

He was always poor. Until the very end of his life, he went on hammering leather and pulling his wax-end. He was ill for quite a short time, then died, serenely and almost joyfully.

* * *

I have opened my family album. Flick through the pages of yours! You will, I hope, find portraits yellowed with the passing of time, but they will certainly have retained a few rays of sunlight.

Greetings to the Sun

Sun of heaven and earth,
sun of the living,
sun of human bodies,
sweet to contemplate and to feel,
light, warmth and life,
warrior too—chasing from one horizon to the other
the fears and specters of the night—
sun, I greet you!

Sun of the dawn and my youth,
white angel, flying gently above the hills,
light, skimming over the ground like a sword,
bringing brightness into our hearts
and wakening song in the trees,
loved by birds and butterflies,
friend of those who get up very early
to earn their daily bread,
monk, singing lauds at daybreak,
sweet promise bringing light and hope,
sun of the dawn, I greet you!

Noonday sun,
sun of our maturity,

sun of achievement and fullness,
seemingly motionless, lasting for ever,
blotting out all shapes in the waves of your light,
cramming the living with your heat
and letting them forget for a while
that they have to die,
you paint the harvest gold and the vineyards red,
royal noonday sun, I greet you!

Evening sun,
sun of my old age,
wounded hero whose blood is running with death,
last kiss of the day before the cold night,
last witness to light before the triumph of night,
monstrance shown to the world,
sun of greetings and farewells,
sun of the evening, I salute you!

Sun of the spirits,
the sun of the body is no more than your misty image,
Word in whom and by whom all the suns of space and time
were created,
Sun of justice, Christ,
I thank you for all the suns of my life—
suns of the morning, of the noonday, of the evening!
Sun of eternity who will never set,
Christ, Sun of justice,
I greet you!

Look Straight into the Mirror!

I would not like this introduction to the evening sun to make my readers think that I have an idyllic view of old age. There has been too much stupid poetry about old age, its sweetness, happiness and tranquillity for me to want to add to it. I would not want to write in this way about old age or about childhood.

"Aging gracefully while waiting for death," said Plantin and Panurge replied to this with cynicism. Old age is not graceful or easy, and the sweetness that it gives us is rather bitter and certainly rare and fragile. One of my friends, a humorist, maintains that we should all resign ourselves to old age because it is the only way that has ever been found of avoiding death. He is right, of course, but it is really no more pleasant to get older than it is to die. "Whoever dies, dies painfully," Villon declared and I would add: "Whoever becomes old, ages painfully," "Whom the gods love die young," Byron wrote, quoting the ancients. Whenever I hear a prominent person who has been invited to open a home for old people singing the praises of old age, I know he is gilding the pill and covering it with sugar so that we shall swallow it more easily.

I would not criticize Simone de Beauvoir for gushing about the beauties of old age. Her well-known book on the subject is concentrated darkness, enough to make one despair. I would only prescribe it as recommended reading matter to old people with a healthy liver, a strong stomach, a well-balanced head, and an unshakably optimistic spirit. I know from reading other books by Madame de Beauvoir that she did not like getting old. She has given all her reasons for being dissatisfied with the aging process with an objectivity that I can only admire. I would not claim that everything that she says is true, but her vision is clear, and her judgment is sound. She does not spare us a single wrinkle. But her book is a study in two-dimensional geometry. It is entirely without the spiritual dimension—those few sun's rays of the kind that shine across even the saddest of Rembrandt's pictures. It is so lacking in that dimension that it is even wrong in its harsh truthfulness and, because of that, dangerous.

No, Madame de Beauvoir, old age may not be very funny, but it does not have to be sad either. Nor do we have to despair about it so long as we look further than the end of our own nose, further than the horizon formed by the walls of the old people's home and, yes, the cemetery. So long, indeed as we look up and see there the evening sun.

Let us not turn back in search of traces of the past that has gone. It is a vain search. Let us look straight ahead and, full of hope, let us look up.

* * *

A great nineteenth-century American, Nathaniel Hawthorne, once wrote a sad, fantastic story called—if I remember correctly—"The Oval Mirror." In this story, some old ladies and gentlemen hold a reunion and, naturally enough, talk about their younger days. One of them claims to have discovered the elixir of youth. He pours some into each glass and they all drink.

They at once become young again and, as they think, beautiful. Their old loves, rivalries, and jealousies, so long buried, reappear. But, as the dancing and the quarreling bring them together and divide them, their real images are reflected in the great "oval mirror" at the end of the room. When the fumes of the drink that they have taken have dissipated, they find themselves in front of the glass and are compelled to see themselves as they really are. They are ridiculous and pitiful old people, drooping, faded, withered, bent and grey. The elixir of youth was only an illusion.

This story is as hard and as cold as the oval mirror itself, but it can teach us a very valuable lesson. So many of my contemporaries are so afraid of old age that they like to imagine that they are still young and do not look straight into the mirror at the image that is also reflected in the eyes of their fellowmen.

I have never been able to like those old people who make a show of being young, those carefully preserved old men who cultivate the last few hairs growing on their head like a garden in winter or those flirtatious old women who display such bony charms. How lacking they are in simplicity, sincerity, and understanding! I know that medical science is able to delay the approach of old age and that beauty treatment can postpone the appearance of its external marks. That is no bad thing! But the time must come when we have to recognize and admit that we are old. Why not, after all? What does it matter? We can, after all, certainly keep our true youth—a youthful heart! How many twenty year olds I have known who were really old people! And how many seventy year olds who have suffered a coronary thrombosis, but who were, in their heart, still twenty!

I have never liked old people who flatter and curry favor with the young with the aim, they say, of keeping in touch with them, but in reality because they themselves need the illusion that they are still young. They make me think of the lustful old men in the book of Daniel, the two elders who desired Susanna when she was bathing, or those ancient alchemists who tried to make an elixir of long life from the blood of the young. When old age comes, we have to understand young people and love them, but this has nothing to do with flattering them and spoiling them. Let us look straight into the mirror, into the eyes of our own image!

* * *

We should, each one of us, practice looking straight at ourselves. If I were to address all old people, I would at once only be speaking generally. My own old age is, after all, only of interest to me and I cannot honestly call it a typical case. As soon as we begin to generalize and to speak about the average old person, everything that we say is at the same time both true and false.

Even if we do generalize, however, and think of old people as a whole, there are many stages and degrees. The worker who has just retired at sixty or sixty-five and the centenarian whose photograph is published in the newspapers are both placed in the category of "old men," but what a difference there is between them! The new medical science of gerontology has given us an insight into the process of aging and the new art of geriatrics has classified the care of the old.

It is possible to uphold the paradoxical argument that we begin to grow old as soon as we are born, but it is quite certain that there is a special moment, usually when we are past fifty and have crossed the wide, level plain of maturity, when we become conscious of getting older, of the process that doctors call senescence. Then, one day, we know that that is it—we have crossed a threshold and we are old in the precise sense of the word.

Then the time comes when we are really very old. First we reach what can be called the "third age" and, if we can hold out, we go on to the "fourth age." At what time in our lives should we place these various thresholds? It is difficult to be precise.

Here we have to generalize and say that old age begins roundabout the sixtieth year of our life and very old age at about seventy-five. There is an age at which we are still young, another when we are young again, and a final age when people declare how astonishingly young we are for our age. These polite euphemisms all point to our growing older. When we reach our second childhood, however, the matter is settled, and it is no longer possible to use euphemisms to describe our condition—we are decrepit, an old wreck, we won't see this year out, and we won't get through the winter.

All the same, as I said before, it is wrong to generalize, because the process of growing old is not identical in each person. There are people, for example, who go calmly down a gentle slope after the age of maturity. Then there are others whose progress is quite different. They get older by fits and starts. They go from cliff to cliff in a series of sudden falls and resting on the level ground—an illness, an accident, a hard blow that they have been unable to resist. What is quite certain is that we should not, as we say in and around Lyon, confuse coming down with going up the hill.

In reality, there is no such thing as old age. It is an abstraction. There is no old age—there are only old people and each old person has his own way of growing old, a way that is in accordance with what used to be known as his idiosyncrasy. All forms of old age have one thing in common, however, and it is this that the mirror shows us without mercy. Old age is an anticipation of death. As we get older, a process of necrosis takes place, medicine tells us, and parts of our body die. Old age, then, is a series of little deaths until one day, when we shall die for good, in good faith. Until that day, we die little by little and bit by bit. We know this, of course, only too well, yet we can never know it quite well enough.

Our Good Old Bodies

As we grow older, we become less and less capable physically. It would be foolish to deny it. Every day brings fresh evidence and we are especially conscious of it in the morning.

"When we are young, our mornings are triumphant," the poet said. Now that we are older, our mornings are alas no longer triumphant. We have to make a great effort to drag our weary body, often full of arthritis, from the bed and face life again.

Let us suppose that the best possible state of affairs exists. We suffer from no chronic complaint and no serious disability. Our hair is white and whispy and we may even be quite without hair. Our skin may be loose and flabby or dry and wrinkled. We certainly have the long sight of old age. Our flesh is either yellow and dull or else red and blotched. One after another, our teeth have left us and, if our mouth is not completely empty, then it is certainly artificially filled.

My grandmother used to say: "Ah, these teeth! You suffer when you put them in. You suffer when you have them and you suffer when you lose them. And when you have no more teeth, you still go on suffering."

And those stiff muscles! Those arms! We can no longer lift the things we used to take up! And our legs do not take us as far as we would like to go or as quickly! And how bent our backs are in old age! And then we are either too thin and bony or too weighed down with that "spare tire." The mirror will not let us deceive ourselves, nor do our inner and outer feelings.

We have to take certain precautions, and these are quite a heavy responsibility. We have to protect ourselves from the cold that seems to penetrate to our poor old bones. We have to remember not to go upstairs too quickly. We have to accept medical and paramedical care. We often want to have a little drink to warm ourselves up or do what we did when we were children—eat a lump of sugar. The very fact that other people are anxious about our old bodies is an irritating reminder of our age.

I knew that I was getting old on the day that a girl got up to give me her place in the Métro in Paris. And this impression was confirmed a little later—and in a very much less edifying way alas—when one of those women who walk the streets by night asked me: "Are you coming, granddad?" I knew it too when I had been talking to my students about the war that I was in, and they asked me innocently: "Which war?" Of course, I replied at once: "The hundred years war."

I think that women—even those who grow old well—suffer more than men in the process, all the more so because they are rudely reminded of it at the menopause and almost without any transition. Apart from a few dandies, men give relatively little attention to their physical beauty and are much more inclined to glorify their strength and their intelligence. Women value their beauty above all and pride themselves on their appearance. However much a woman may do "to repair the irreparable ravages of the years," as the poet said, and however hard she may try to deceive herself, the moment of truth will come sooner or later.

The beautiful queen in the story of Snow White discovered in front of the mirror that she was no more than a witch with a hooked nose. Despite all her care and attention, the beautiful, perfect woman with her tall, slim figure must inevitably become coarser, thinner, more shrivelled and even, like a tree in winter, stunted.

All women are bound, as they become old, to feel what Villon's beautiful Heaumière felt and deeply regret the gradual failure of their body, its slow decline: "female body that is so tender, sleek and gracious." A friend of mine who died when she was still very young told me that she was not sorry because old age frightened her. She was a simple young woman and not at all vain, but she knew that, when you were old, "you were no longer pretty" and this confession came from her innermost depths, her feminine instinct.

We should not forget that these are cases of old people who are not chronically sick or disabled. We should remember those who are ill. If we have avoided the worst illnesses of the middle years—coronary thrombosis, nervous depression, stomach ulcers—we have the choice of the illnesses of old age. These include, as we all know, arthritis, rheumatism, bronchitis, catarrh of various kinds and, because I am not a doctor, I cannot list them all. I am, however, bound to mention one trouble that may happen to any man in old age—the enlargement of the prostate. Many of these troubles are not painful or even very serious, but they are embarrassing and humiliating. Each one on its own may be relatively insignificant, but all together these little ailments combine to form one great disorder to which we resign ourselves in the knowledge that it will probably be with us to the end. The outward sign is the old person's stick. As the Sphynx told Oedipus, the old man is the animal that walks on three legs.

Oh my body! My old body! My good companion on the way or in the struggle, how you call me to order! In pain, stiff in the joints, heavy, out of breath, coughing—how demanding you are! In the past, when my muscles moved freely and easily inside the covering of my skin, I did what I wanted to do with you—or almost what I wanted. Now, however, I have to do what you want. I have to use you economically. I have to pamper you and wrap you up in cotton wool. You remind me of a very old car, repainted, touched up, adjusted, readjusted, refurbished and still able to go, puffing and wheezing, more or less by habit. There is only one difference between me and the old car—I cannot find any spare parts in the garage for my old body. Sometimes my thoughts go back to earlier days and you remind me of one of those old cabhorses that have to be flogged before they put one foot in front of the other and which give the impression that they would collapse if the shafts of the cab were taken away from them.

And yet I love you, my dear old body. The more tattered you become, the more I love you, because you preserve what is left of my life and through you I am still plugged in to the beauty of the world. One day, I know, we shall have to say goodbye to each other, when my heart ceases to beat. But I hope to find you again, after the resurrection, full of glory.

Our Good Old Minds

Physically, we inevitably become less in old age. Do we also suffer an intellectual decline? Some people clearly break down mentally and others enter first an impenetrable mist and then the darkness of night. But these are extreme cases. We can to some extent generalize about them, but not about most old people.

We should never forget that, in the case of a great number of people, the intellect becomes fixed at quite an early age, often soon after adolescence. Although they may continue to be capable of acquiring knowledge, they cease almost entirely to evolve. A person who is rigid at adolescence will remain rigid in old age. A young person who is less able is unlikely to become brilliant as the years go by. It would be wrong to enter on the debit side of the account of old age a liability that goes back to youth and an early closing of the mind. Closed minds, it would seem, never open.

Intellectual development varies a great deal according to the individual, his whole environment, and the circumstances of his life. We have only to think of the world of literature. Many young writers—Rimbaud, Lautréamont, and Radiguet, for example—have said everything that they have to say before they are twenty. Other equally gifted writers go on creating until the end of their lives, fully in control of their thoughts and words. Goethe was one of these Olympian figures. Victor Hugo was another. The Hugo of the latest poems—*Dieu, Satan,* and *La fin de Satan*—is much greater than the brilliant young author of the *Odes et Ballades.* One of my friends, Colonel Roullet, who wrote for the *Chronique Sociale* and the *Vie Intellectuelle,* retained the youthful flexibility of his mind until he ceased to write at the age of ninety. His style and his ideas were those of a man of forty.

Similar examples can easily be found in the sphere of politics. Two great old men come immediately to mind. Clemenceau saved France in the First World War and Adenauer, who took charge of Germany when the country was at its lowest point, was the chief author of the German economic miracle. And you can think what you like about General de Gaulle, except that his mind was like Colonel Ramollet's.

The fact remains, however, that most people achieve most at the age of maturity, that is, between the ages of twenty and sixty-five. Before this time, they are still learning their grade. It is only later that they reach the peak of maturity. When they were young, they were in full possession of their adult powers, to begin with, perhaps, only as a potential. Old age may lead them to give up certain responsibilities that they feel will be too heavy for them. It need not, however, completely extinguish the flame of their mind. Indeed, a change of activity may even revive it.

Our intelligence is not, after all, a single faculty. It is rather a complex of dispositions and its power varies according to the individual and his circumstances. It is a mistake to do what so many French people do because they are, consciously or unconsciously, disciples of Voltaire, namely to confuse intelligence with brilliance, that gift that is conferred by a classical literary education. It is quite possible to be brilliant in this way and yet fundamentally stupid or even superficial.

Our intelligence is also closely associated with such factors as reason, memory, imagination, and culture, our openness to new ideas, and the continuous process by which we become adapted to the changing reality of life. I am sure that an old person's reason is equal to that of a young manor woman, and I would not hesitate to upset a few prejudices, perhaps, by claiming that it goes beyond that of a young person. Habit and experience are powerful factors acting in favor of reason, the mechanical functioning of which improves with the passage of time. It cannot, however, function in a vacuum and it would be a mistake to think that it can be developed without any help from the imagination or the memory.

It is here that the old person benefits from his experience. I do not mean technical experience in this case. Our technical experience soon becomes obsolescent, as the economists would say—they, no doubt, would find the simple term "out of date" outmoded. No, by "experience" here, I mean simply human experience. "He's young and he doesn't know," Maurice Chevalier used to sing—and he was himself a good example of old age. The old man, however, knows, with a knowledge that nourishes his reason.

Memory, on the other hand, is an entirely different question. An old person's memory is never as good as it was when he was young. It is, however, valuable to note how capriciously and bafflingly the memory behaves in old age. We remember what we think that we have forgotten, and our minds are full of events that happened in our childhood and adolescence but are now clothed in warm, bright, and often very deceptive garments. At the same time, we often forget what has just happened or what we have to do here and now. Is this forgetfulness due to a failure of memory or to simple inattention? I think it is the second, because old people are notoriously absent-minded. When I wonder where I have put my glasses and then, after looking for them, find them on my nose, this is not so much a lapse of memory as inattentiveness. Dreaming of something or other, I had not been following the thread of my actions. Every old man has an opposite side to his personality that is knowledgable but does not know itself.

As our body wears out, it has effects on our mind, that complex human structure in which everything is contained and conditioned. We cannot work as much or as well as we used to, nor can we make decisions as quickly as we did. This is particularly painful for those of us who have always worked hard. But if we want to grow old beautifully and in peace, we must recognize it as a fact. As a rule, it is not suitable for us old people to have too much authority, but this does not mean that we should become critical inspectors of work that has been done long ago or specialists in matters that have long been shelved. Our task is to counsel and to make our experience and wisdom available.

As we get older, we find it difficult and even painful to acquire new knowledge or skills and to adapt to new situations. This is unfortunately something that has to be done at every stage of life, even when we are no longer young, but age does not make it any easier. We have to make an effort to understand what young people seem to understand without difficulty and even then we often do not succeed in understanding. As Royer-Collard told Vigny, who had come to see him and asked him whether he knew his work, "You should know, sir, that there is an age when one reads and an age when one rereads." This was not a kind thing to say, but it was and still is true.

The old man, then, is at the stage of life when he rereads and when he reduces what he does not know to what he knows and the present to the past. It is, however, possible to combat this intellectual paralysis—so long, of course, as one is aware of it. We can, then, adapt ourselves to a new reality which has many surprising and even deeply shocking features. We had, when we were younger, to adapt ourselves to increasing road traffic and faster and more dangerous driving. Why, then, should we not be able to accept new and different ideas?

We should not despair, after all, of our good old minds. They will always be good and faithful servants and more readily available to us than we are sometimes prepared to think, provided that we do not ask more of them than they are able to give. We should not be in too much of a hurry to call ourselves old fools and to think that we are only fit to be thrown away, like a ticket that has been punched. Our minds have not been extinguished. They have simply changed with our age. We have to learn how to use them as they are now.

Our Poor Old Hearts

Just as fountains often become clogged with lime and function less and less well, so too do our muscles and bones become stiffer as we get older. Our minds too become slower. Our hearts, on the other hand, become softer, more tender and more sensitive. Our emotional life becomes harder in maturity, but old age brings a rejuvenation.

There are, of course, old people who are insensitive and selfish, wrapped up in themselves, bad tempered old men and malevolent old witches. It you look closely at their whole life-history, however, you will certainly find that old age has simply emphasized the cruder aspects of an attitude that has always been there. The selfish old man certainly did not wait until he was sixty before he became engrossed in himself and his own little happiness. The irritable, sharp old woman was almost always a bitter, waspish young one. Age simply hardens hearts that were originally made of stone. We have the old age that we deserve.

Most old people—there are exceptions, of course—do not display the enthusiasm of the young, that flame that rises up and dies so quickly. This apparent coldness is quite easy to understand. Old people have seen and experienced too much. They have had too many illusions and have been disillusioned too many times to be so easily caught in the trap. All human experience is to some extent bitter. The longer that experience lasts, the more acid it becomes.

But the old man is usually more tender than the middle-aged person. He is able to show more simple goodness. The great indulgence of grandparents is proverbial. It has its origin to some extent in weakness and to a great extent in goodness and tenderness. Old hearts have a hidden treasure of affection that young and adult hearts either cannot see or else can only exploit too much.

Many old people cry easily. This is well known and has been the subject of rather cruel laughter. It has, for example, been said in the Church that a parish priest is ready to be made a monsignor when he begins to cry every time he reads the diocesan newsletter. Being moved to tears of pity, however, is not the same as being soft-witted. Other old people remain dry-eyed even in the greatest grief. So much so that one would think their tears had dried up at their source. These old men and women are not necessarily the least sensitive. They are probably the ones who have suffered too much.

We should not harden ourselves to reject this excess of emotion in old people and we should certainly not be ashamed of it in ourselves. It is a clear proof that our heart is still young although our body may be old. Our heart is still that of a child. Let us rather take advantage of it so that a few rays of the evening sun shine in our direction—like a baby trying to catch the light that shines into his room in his little hands.

It looks, then, as though we must expect to suffer. This is a ransom that we have to pay. Trivialities that did not trouble us when we were younger now ruffle and even bruise us deeply. We are hurt by apparent indifference, forgetfulness, or hardness. But how many other trivial things bring us joy! A young woman's smile, a young man's politeness, a child's kiss, a neighbor's friendly joke, a meeting with an old friend or simply the beauty of a flower, the romping of a kitten or the noisy advances of a dog!

I often travel by plane. I freely confess that the care I receive from the air hostesses because of my bad legs always moves me very much. They are only doing what they have to do, cynics tell me, adding sometimes, "They are paid for it." But no, they are doing much more than they have to and they do it better. They have that generosity that only women have and, as Proudhon said, they always go further than justice. A nice face, attractive and cheerful, perhaps, well, it makes a great difference. And if I were gloomy and complaining, a thoroughly miserable old man, I would not receive the treatment, perhaps. But, after all, what does it matter? I just notice what happens and I am glad about it.

So let us thank God, who has let our poor old hearts grow young again in old age, so that we can love better. Even if we have to suffer for it sometimes, it is always good to love.

The Song of Acceptance

Lord, Ancient of Days,
eternal youth, eternal maturity, eternal old age
eternity of infinite love—
I thank you for bringing me to my present age.
Here I have no future and am close to eternity;
I can look back at my past
as Moses, from Mount Nebo, saw the promised land.

I thought for a long time that I would die young
and this filled me with a kind of joy.
Death several times arranged to meet me
and I waited several times,
sometimes at peace, sometimes in agony.
Death did not keep the appointment.
May your will be done,
king of the centuries,
Lord of the hour.

I accept, good Lord, the share of life that you have so carefully
measured out for me
and I will give it back to you when you want it.
I accept old age, because you have given it to me.

I accept the evening sun, because it reflects in creation your uncreated light.
I accept it as I accepted my youth and my maturity,
with the same joy.

I accept this old, weak, sick body,
this shaky carcass,
this tortured, suffering mass of flesh and bones
that is so difficult to drag along.
It still has enough strength to go where you want me to go
and if it must at some time cease to move,
that lack of movement will be a step toward you.
May it go on serving me so that I may serve you.
I ask you this through our Lord Jesus Christ,
your Son, whose body passed through death.

I accept this rusting and drying of the mind.
So long as enough is left for me to know you and make you known,
I shall be happy.
Let me remain curious and let my spirit be available.
I ask you this through Jesus Christ our Lord,
your Word, the light in whom I see your light.

I accept the young and tender heart you leave me,
that heart which, more than ever, needs love to give and love to receive.
Even if it has suffered too much and no longer trusts the loves of man,
it knows your love, Lord, whose name is love.
Keep it wide open, available to every suffering and every joy.

I ask you this through our Lord Jesus Christ,
gentle and humble of heart,
whose heart was opened by the centurion's lance
and pours out love forever.

Amen

Rejected by Modern Civilization

Our modern civilization has no love for children or for old folk—both spoil our fun. This dislike, of course, is not expressed aloud and indeed, it may not even be consciously felt. What happens is that we do what the psychologists call compensate for it—we spoil children and, especially when there is an election in the offing and old people's votes begin to count, we sing a few hymns in their honor.

It is important to be—or at least to seem to be—young now. Youth is exalted—and exploited—by modern publicity and propaganda. In this chorus of modern society, the old man is out of tune. He is a *memento mori*—remember, man, that you must die! He is like those skulls and shinbones that used to be placed at the entrance to graveyards. *Hodie mihi, cras tibi*—me today, you tomorrow! This is what you will soon be, inexorably.

When a little old granny walks past with a wrinkled russet apple face, clutching a bag with a few meager purchases, the fine lady with smooth, carefully made up skin shudders. And when a young man hears his grandfather tell him for the thousandth time about the battle of Verdun in the First World War or his adventures with the Resistance in the Second, he has a dark feeling of apprehension—will he be like that one day?

So, in order not to see these disagreeable old people, we group them all together in homes, shelters, or even districts with a predominantly aged population. Oh, this concentration may not come about deliberately, but it certainly comes about. After all, those modern lepers, the mentally ill—are they not concentrated in psychiatric wards? And students in the university campus? And the dead in great urban cemeteries? One more or one less concentration—what does it matter?

Consumer society has no use for old people. They no longer buy or consume, and they no longer produce anything. They are no longer useful. They spend very little. With the present continuous devaluation of money, our economy is always looking ahead to the future and reduces its unproductive aged to the bare subsistence level or even to below the subsistence level. They live on fixed incomes, pensions, or allowances. In the social structures of our modern world, the old ones form a large part of the neoproletariat. Some are dedicated to a life of misery and public or private social security. Others live in a permanent state of financial embarrassment that is very close to misery. Only a small minority are able to some degree to avoid these evils—those who, when they were younger, took precautions to lay the foundations for a comfortable retirement and could afford then to save for it. If war breaks out or there is a great crisis, it is always the old people who suffer worst, because of their economic weakness.

Twentieth-century society is characterized by the structure known as the nuclear family—man and wife and a few young children. Dwelling houses are built to accommodate this kind of family—only a few, usually very small rooms. There is no place in such homes for the old folks of the family. Granddad is just in the way—both in the material space and in the psychological space. Once again we find him consigned to a concentration of people of his own age, either in specially designed homes for the aged or in older houses used for the purpose or in a decayed part of the town, where the rooms and flats are older than he is, but are at least cheap, even though they are too big for him now. How often old people live at the very top of high urban blocks—as if we wanted them to be close to the heaven that is waiting for them and wanted to spare them the journey there!

I recently watched a television program about old people who had sought refuge on the Côte d'Azur, drawn there clearly by the sun's rays. In search of a perpetual springtime, they had found nothing but misery and loss.

The misery of poor old people! The Little Brothers of the Poor are not deterred by hundreds of stairs and regularly visit as many old folk as they can. They could certainly tell us a great deal about the wretchedness of old age! Even if there is no material misery, there is always the loneliness and the sad feeling that you no longer count and have no further purpose or function. Even the Church, which ought to be the Church of the poor and, therefore, the Church of the lonely and abandoned ones, sometimes gives the impression—through some of its priests—that it is indifferent to and even scornful of old age. I know a very old lady who knew no one to whom she could talk and went to confession, to confide her misery in the priest but was literally chased away by the latter, who, if he was not hard-hearted, was certainly lacking in imagination. Luckily, much more attention is being given nowadays in the Church to the spiritual care of the aged.

And those old people's homes! Simone de Beauvoir has given us a very unflattering description and I read what she had to say when I was engaged in social activities with the aged. I would say that she generalized too much, but did not exaggerate. She was even refused admission into the home at Nanterre. That is one of the worst places of all where old folk are sent to die. The only advantage that it can offer is that its guests are spared, by God's mercy, some of the time they would otherwise spend in purgatory!

I have visited some of these large homes, in which old people are subjected to a discipline that present-day soldiers and boarding-school pupils would not accept—and rightly! The inmates of so many of these homes are restricted to a few square yards "living space" and are forced to be inactive. The community in which they live is an artificial one. . . . I have also been in the smaller, local homes, where there is sometimes a better family atmosphere, but often an autocratic and bad-humored rule. I am now at last able to understand that old tramp who always spent the winter in whatever home would take him, but, as soon as the first swallows arrived, would set off on the road again. He was a wise, practical old man.

It is true that the Little Sisters of the Poor, whom I love because I have learned to appreciate their work, have houses for the old. Simone de Beauvoir has not written about their homes—I hope because she did not know about them. If she had met the Sisters, she might have been less pessimistic, especially since they have improved their methods and their lodgings in recent years.

The fact remains, however, that the old people are still concentrated, even in the homes of the Little Sisters, and obliged to live on top of each other, without any contact with young people or people of mature years. And, of course, the Sisters themselves have fewer and fewer vocations. But how can they expect very many? It is hardly an attractive career—dedicating the whole of one's life to old people who are so often grumpy and bad-tempered or even worse, half-paralyzed in mind or body. Our consumer society does not prepare people for this kind of situation.

I don't want to paint too black a picture. I know a great deal of progress has been made. There are old people's homes providing much smaller units and letting even the oldest inmates remain much more independent. Allowances too are better than they were in the past, and old people no longer die of hunger. I have already pointed to a few of the services to old people and, of course, there are many others. A great deal is done, for example, by the Society of Saint Vincent de Paul! All the same, how far we are from giving back to the oldest members of our society everything that they have done for us!

I do not want to contrast the past and the present in an artificial way. But it cannot be denied that, in the past and especially in rural communities, the old man had a scarcity value. The world changed very slowly and his experience was very valuable. He was a kind of walking encyclopedia bound in wrinkled skin. It was an honor to be called an old man or an elder. The Arabic word "sheik" means "old man" and the French word "monsieur" corresponds to the Latin *mi senior,* my elder. (Lest the ladies should feel outdone, let them be reassured that "madame" means *mea domina,* my sovereign lady.)

But nowadays life has changed and old age is exposed to the public gaze. The word "old" has become a term of abuse—"you old fool!" or, "you stupid old woman!" We should not, of course, imagine that life was always sunny for old people in the past, even in the days of the patriarchal family. But there was no social problem of old age of the kind that we have today, simply because there were so few old people, and the family structure allowed different generations to live together, perhaps not in perfect harmony, but rubbing along.

Modern civilization is strangely illogical. Medicine has made such advances that people live longer and there are many more old folk. But now that we have so many of them with us, we do not really know what to do with them. The problem of a world overpopulated with old people is a directly social one. It cannot be solved in isolation. It certainly cannot be solved unless those who are principally concerned—the old people themselves—are consulted. They have more to contribute toward a solution of their own problem than simply making a complaint or a claim. What are required are solidarity, mutual aid, and joint action. Old people—rejected by the prosperous society, the new proletariat—unite!

But It Is Good To Be Old!

"But it is good to be old!"

What do you mean? After all those cruel analyses of old age, you can say such a silly thing! What cheek you have! Or perhaps you just don't really understand.

"Not at all! At one time when I was young, I used to sing with my young German friends: 'Wir sind jung und das ist schön!' and I don't regret it. I thank the Lord that I was young and that it was good. Now old age has come upon me and I sing: 'We are old and it is good!' "

"Why, then?"

"Because it is good to be alive. Because it is good to be a man. At all times of life."

"Do you really want me to believe that? You limp along. You are always coughing. You take pills for this and tablets for that. You have injections and you go regularly for massage. You are one of the best customers of the welfare state. And you claim to be happy!"

"I don't claim to be happy. I have never claimed to be happy, even when I was twenty and went about in a state of gentle melancholy. All I say is that it is good to have a body, even though it is a bit worn. It lets me remain in touch with the beauty of the world. I need glasses, but I can see the light and that, as the ancient Greeks used to say, is sweet. I am a bit hard of hearing, but I can still listen to music and hear the wind in the trees. My stomach is not proof against everything that enters it, but I can still drink a glass of good old wine from time to time. Believe me, the rarer and more threatened my experiences are, the more pleasant I find them. I am alive and I am open to everything that life gives me. And it gives me an abundance of things."

"You may be right, There was a time when you used to work without a break for fourteen or fifteen hours a day. We used to envy you! And now you have retired—don't you find inactivity tiring?"

"Life is different now. I have retired, but I have almost as much to keep me busy as I did during the active period of my life. I work more slowly, and it is not so easy, but I can choose what to do and do it when I want to. I admit I am less open to new ideas, but I have the past at my disposal."

"Oh, the past! Let's talk about that! It's time to chew over all those bitter experiences!"

"No . . . I don't chew over bitter herbs. My memories are sweet and aromatic. My life wasn't all failure and sin. There was a lot of happiness in it. It is the hours that were full of light that I relive. I see again in my mind's eye those I loved and have lost. Strange and happy transformations take place in the memory—what was hard at the time is softened in recollection. When I meet my wartime friends again, my comrades in the Resistance and the men I knew in prison and we talk about our life together, even if we don't say so in so many words, we know they were the good old days."

"But don't you sometimes feel chilled by the wind of loneliness?"

"Even though we may not seem to be, we are alone all through our lives. We just become more aware of it as we get older—as death takes those who surround us away. We look more and more like ancient oak trees in a forest clearing. But a few old friends remain and, if we really take the trouble to look, we can always find younger ones. I can love better than I used to! Less passionately, but my love is disinterested now. I have learned from experience that love is giving myself to others. And then, of course, I can always go back to books. They can always give me friends who are available when I need them—Don Quixote and Sancho Panza, Father Brown, Chesterton, Bernanos, and so many others."

"You are very wise."

"No, not really. I just try to be wise. If we are not wise when we are old, whenever shall we be? I've lived too long to have any illusions, of course. I no longer have those wild surges of enthusiasm that I had when I was young, nor do I feel as self-satisfied as I did in middle life. But I can see further and more clearly, both into the past and into the future. I know how weak man is, but I don't love him any less or condemn him for it, because I am weak too. Life is, I think, like a tree heavy with fruit. I can taste this fruit—with restraint, so that I avoid indigestion—but I don't want to keep it all to myself and prefer to share it with others. Or, if you like, it is like a rose. I can smell its perfume as I pass by, but I leave it on its stem, so that other passersby can smell it too. Maurice du Plessis wrote once: 'I've swigged wine and sniffed roses. I've picked the flower of many a kiss. None of this excites me any more.' I can't agree with him. I've often drunk too much—and I've suffered for it the next morning. But I've never lost my taste for food and drink and the world strikes me as just as beautiful as it did when I first discovered it. It is probably this experience of old age that inspired Victor Hugo, who was often very far from wise, to write: 'With a young man's eyes we see the flame, but with the eyes of old age we see the light.'"

"Your wisdom is very Epicurian for a confessed Christian. As one of our friends back in Lyon said, in sepulcral tones: 'You would do better to think about preparing for a good death.'"

"I am thinking about it, my dear old friend. Of course I am. But I can't understand why the thought of death should prevent me from living or why the closeness of death should stop my enjoying the evening sun. Why shouldn't I value the flowers that God puts in our way? Even the simplest—the daisies, the violets, and the buttercups? It's a way of doing homage to his beauty and his goodness. Pascal told us how to make good use of illness. Why should we not take advantage of old age, which is no more of an illness than youth, but is another stage of life's journey?"

"The last stage!"

"All the more reason to take advantage of it! We're climbing up to the last inn and we reach it at sunset. So long as day lasts, let's be open to the light. Getting old may be hard, but it is good to be old!"

A Little Prayer

Lord, you have shared our life in all its stages and you experienced old age.
Do not let me become a grumpy old man,
always complaining, quarreling, and criticizing,
a burden to himself and others.
Let me go on laughing and smiling,
even though I show the world a toothless mouth
or discolored dentures.
Let me keep my sense of humor,
so that I can put people—and myself—in the right place,
laugh at my own faults and joke about my sufferings.
Make me, Lord, a smiling old man,
who, though he can no longer give much to his brothers,
can at least give them a little joy.

Lord, you put a heart of flesh in my breast
to love with and to be loved,
a heart like the pierced heart of your Son.
Do not let me become a selfish old man,
bent over his little self like a smoldering peat fire,
shut inside the four walls of his own limitations
and tormented by fear of loss and cold draughts.

Keep my heart open
and my hand always ready to shake other hands
and open to give.
Make me a generous old man, Lord,
sharing his threepence with those who only have one
and the flowers in his garden with those who have no garden,
stroking dogs and cats on his way,
smiling at little children
and crumbling bread for the sparrows in the park.

Lord, you are eternally present.
Do not let me become an old man who lives in the past,
always talking about the good old times when it was never cold
and disliking the present time of young people, when it is
always raining.
Make me live my past again with happiness,
but let me also love and understand the present,
which is yours, like the past and the future.
Let me be an old man, Lord, who has not forgotten his youth
and who makes others feel young.

Lord, you have established the seasons of the year and the
seasons of man's life.
Let me be a man of all seasons.
I don't ask you for happiness,
because I know only too well that no season will bring it,
not even spring.
But I do ask you that the last season of my life may be fine,
so that it will bear witness to your beauty.

Amen

Resignation or Acceptance?

Old age has arrived. I have, I think, described it without much pleasure, but also without bitterness. I am not irritatingly optimistic about its coming, nor am I so pessimistic that it affects my liver. But it is knocking at my door and, whether I like it or not, I have simply to say: "Come in!" In what tone of voice should I say those two syllables? With resignation or with acceptance?

Many people would say: with resignation, because there is no other way. To resist would be folly, so let us be resigned.

I do not like resignation, either as a word or as an idea. It suggests passivity, whimpering, complaining, and forcing oneself. We have to be resigned to old age, that is all. Body and soul, guts and all—everything is getting older. Resignation has been presented to us as a great Christian virtue. This is a mistake and it may even be a fraud. Christ did not resign himself to death in the garden of olives—he accepted the Father's will. He was not resigned while on the cross—he offered himself with outstretched arms. I do not think that resignation is a virtue as such, a simple human virtue, because the greatness of man is to be found in struggle.

That is why I prefer the term acceptance. I accept what I cannot prevent. I cling actively to God's will. I do not submit to my fate—I accept it. I take it on myself and, because old age is inextricably part of my destiny as a man, I go forward to meet it with joy. I do not let myself be dragged along by my old age—I carry it myself.

Accepting old age is accepting myself as a person, accepting my human condition, which requires me to go through all the ages of life until, at the end, I encounter death. The ancient Greeks knew what they were talking about when they used the words mortal and man as synonyms. My human condition is my greatness and my pride. "Only a little below the angels," the psalmist said—and so much above the animals! I cannot accept that condition with reservations or subject to qualifications. It has to be taken or left. I take it—the whole human condition including old age and death.

Just as there are some men and women who do not accept their own sex—but try as they will, they will never change it!—so too there are human beings who refuse their condition and the limits it imposes on them. Perhaps they would prefer to be angels, set free from their body, the weight of the flesh and its mortality. Or perhaps they would rather be animals, in happy ignorance of the future. What they cannot accept is the encounter between the animal and the spiritual that characterizes man.

In one sense, such people are not wrong. Man goes beyond man. He is, after all, open to eternity and infinity. He contains more than pure humanity. Saint John of the Cross called him a god in flower. If, however, he is to reach divinity, he must go along the way of acceptance of his humanity, just as Christ, the Word of God, accepted mortal flesh and became man, showing us the way of the cross and the Resurrection.

To accept old age is to accept time. We are creatures of time. We are born, we live, we move and we die in time. Our limits are defined by time and space. But that time is also in contact with eternity, because we carry within us, even now, the seeds of the new life that is eternal life. Time wears us away and condemns us to old age, but it is also the way along which we go toward eternity.

Lord Jesus, God and man, I accept my humanity with you. I accept old age, but I offer it to you as I offered you in the past my youth and my mature years. Halleluiah!

* * *

When I speak of joyful acceptance, I do not mean something laughable. I do not need to say again that old age is not funny. In fact, I wonder what stage in life is really laughable or funny. Not even childhood is, although much of the poetic fantasy that we weave around it is very false.

Accepting old age is also accepting what it brings along with it. We have to accept, for example, the poverty that goes with old age. Even if we do not have to struggle with real misery or put up with shortage of money like an iron collar, we are bound to have less to live on and we have to count our pennies, make economies, do without, and plan more carefully. This is the reason for that more-or-less unconscious meanness from which so many old people suffer. Molière's miserly Harpagon could never be painted with the features of a young man!

Younger people inevitably think: The old ones don't need as much as we do. And that is relatively speaking true. It is a general truth. We usually don't have the expense of a young family. We eat much less as a rule. We end by wearing our old clothes and our old shoes and we keep our old furniture. We have fewer demands with regard to entertainment. Reading, listening to the radio, or watching television are normally enough for us, and we are content to talk to friends or to go for a walk.

But when you have been well off or even if you have only had sufficient to live on, you suffer if you begin to feel the pinch.

Nonetheless, if we accept the poverty that accompanies old age and accept it joyfully, we shall be set free from our artificial needs, our vain worldliness and the lure of self-aggrandisement. It will bring us close to the poor whom God loves and close to the life of the gospel.

To accept old age is to accept the weakness of old age. If only youth were knowledgable and old age were able to achieve! But youth does not yet know and old age can no longer achieve! We have all enjoyed moments of full experience, when our knowledge and our ability were in a state of perfect equilibrium. Caught up in action, we were not even conscious of those moments and they passed—like that!

Nothing is harder on the one hand, for the man who has been a worker or for the woman who was an active, good housekeeper, than to see everything that has to be done and not to be able to do it. We old people try—but we lack the strength and have to abandon the attempt. I often think of the regrets that old sporting champions must feel. Those regrets seem to me to symbolize the sorrow of all old people.

On the other hand, a joyful acceptance of our own weakness will, if we are able to banish envy, help us to rejoice in the strength of those who follow us and will replace us—our children and our disciples. I remember what an old teacher once said to me. She spoke with pride about a famous person, saying that she had taught him to read. . . . In the course of my own life, I have contributed to the education of several young people and it is consoling to me to see them carry on with tasks that I have begun, even though they do not go about it in the way that I would. After all, it was never my intention to make them into well-assembled pieces of machinery or disciples who simply repeated my words. I wanted them to be free! If they made use of their freedom, I would be successful. And then, our weakness, accepted joyfully, also turns us toward our unfailing source of strength—our Lord. Whether we like it or not, we have to get rid of that often stinking self-sufficiency of our adult years. Is it really wrong?

Accepting old age is also accepting loneliness or dependence or both together, because we can be very lonely when we are most cared for by others. However surrounded we are by loving people, we are alone, for those of our own generation, with whom we can speak as equals and exchange mutual reminiscences, become fewer each day. And those who love and care for us are aware of our weakness and are anxious about us, so they surround us with precautions that keep us in a state of dependence. Little children depend on women—usually their mothers, of course—and so do old people—they depend on female relatives, nurses, and nuns.

There was a touching passage in an American thriller that I read years ago, describing how a Sicilian gangster, free after a long term of imprisonment, found his old age painful because his daughter, who cared for him, was so protective. He, who had been a hardened killer and the head of a patriarchal family, was powerless and disarmed. I also remember the secret irritation of the aged Jolyon Forsyte in Galsworthy's *Saga,* brought about by the precautions taken by those near to him in an attempt to prolong his life by a few days or even hours.

The granddaughter, who made her first steps when we held her hand, is transformed into a mother-hen, anxious and authoritarian: "Be careful! Do this! Don't do that! Don't forget your scarf! Take your pills now! . . ." And the poor old mother sees her grown up son assure her with lavish words that he certainly does not believe himself: "Don't worry, mother. Everything will be all right! I'll take care of it!"

There is a good deal of pain in this reversal of roles. It is hardly surprising that the old person should sometimes reply with a grunt or with obstinate silence. It is by this response that he tries to regain his earlier independence.

I have not mentioned any really unhappy cases of loneliness and dependence. All my examples are happy enough ones, in which the old person is surrounded by people who love him and enslave him with a surfeit of care and attention.

An acceptance of one's dependence may, however, be a cause of joy. It will prove that those near to us love us, even though they love us clumsily and leave us little freedom. It will remind us of human solidarity and the love of God that is grafted on to that solidarity. For our part, we can react to those loving attentions that keep us prisoner by little acts that show that we are still free. We can, for example, smile, make a joke, give a present, or do a kindness. People gossiped, complained, and quarreled in the big working-class homes of an earlier generation, but there was also a tremendous solidarity. It was not emphasized or expressed orally, but it existed. The middle-aged mother, for example, did shopping and small tasks for the grandfathers and grandmothers and sometimes even all their housework. In return, the old ones looked after the kids. This is not a fairy story—it is what happened when I was young.

There is nothing humiliating in being dependent. We simply have to accept it. It is natural, like the association of the blind and the paralyzed.

* * *

Acceptance is a key-word in Christian living and indeed in life as such. It is the consent of the incarnate Word to the Father's will and the consent of the Virgin to the word of the angel.

The best pagan thinkers knew what it meant. The Stoics believed that destiny guided those who consented and dragged along those who refused. I have often reminded myself of this teaching when times were hard, although I do not think of destiny in a fatalistic sense. Acceptance is not following the river downstream like a dying dog. It is not resignation. It is, in a word, wanting. Let us accept our old age! If we do not, our life will not be in accordance with human nature.

Staying Young in Spite of Everything

"We must accept old age. We have to stay young in spite of everything—until the end."

"Clearly you are not afraid of speaking in paradoxes or contradicting yourself. Are you making fun of me?"

"God forbid! I am not contradicting myself! And what you call a paradox is simply the same truth seen from two different points of view."

"You make me mad. What on earth do you mean?"

"I certainly don't mean that an old person should try to preserve the illusion of youth. If I had meant this, would I have invited old people to look in the mirror? That would be like claiming that I could do the pole vault when in fact I can hardly put one foot in front of the other."

"You would fall, you mean?"

"You have taken the words out of my mouth. Even if it seems to console us a little, illusion is always dangerous. I don't think old people should imitate youth or play at being young."

"If that is what you mean, then I think you are right. When old people pretend to be young, they make other old people laugh at them and young ones despise them. A writer who is forgotten nowadays, but who had some talent, Jean Rameau, wrote a novel about an old painter who felt himself going downhill, but wanted to go on seeming young. He always wanted to be in fashion—jumping on every bandwagon, as they say today. When a young artist or would-be artist showed him any picture at all, no matter how bad, he would exclaim: 'That is stupendous! A masterpiece! It puts everything to shame!' He lied to young people. He lied to himself. And in the depths of his heart, he knew he was lying."

"Jean Rameau must have been a simpleton! But for once, simple though he was, he was right. I agree with him—and with you."

"And I can't stand those women who are past it, but who play at being girls—even little girls—with their clothes, their manners and the way they talk. Their mental age is usually the same as the chronological age they are pretending to be."

"I'm still in agreement with you!"

"But I'm still mystified. I know what you don't mean, but I still don't understand what you do mean."

"Oh, it's very easy. Have you ever seen the sky when it is full of rain-clouds and quite dark, but one little corner of it is still bright blue."

"Of course I have. Well?"

"Well! That is like staying young when you are really old!"

"I can't think in images. I can only deal with thoughts."

"Do you mean that you're not happy with my little image? We can talk in abstractions if you prefer. We don't become old all at once, the whole of us—old in two or three movements, as teachers of Swedish drill used to say. No, certain parts of us become old and others don't. We have to keep the parts that don't become old so quickly young for as long as we can."

"Give me an example."

"Your body can be full of aches and pains and your bones old and arthritic, but your mind can be quite free. You may have a weak heart, but it can still be spiritually young. Why should I let what is still young and alive in me become old and stiff with the part that is aging? You were speaking just now about childish old ladies. Well, I know others who are not ashamed of being old, but who are still enviably and even frighteningly lively and vigorous in mind and spirit!"

"I'm beginning to understand."

"There are also values which we always associate with youth, but which do not belong exclusively to young people. Sincerity, for example, the ability to be indignant about the ugly, unpleasant things in life or to be enthusiastic about what is true, good, and beautiful, a sense of justice and an easiness in human relationships and in making friends. . . . Young people are much more spontaneous in their expression of these qualities than we are, of course, and that is normal enough. We old ones have, after all, learnt the bitter lesson of experience. We should let them have a monopoly, however, a full concession with government approval. I have met old nuns whose spirits were remarkably young. (There was only one task, incidentally, that was more difficult than estimating the age of a man and that was calculating the age of a sister, at the time when they used to wear a habit and veil.) But some of them were eighty or more, yet they still smiled like young women! I still know old men who are younger in every way than many young men, and I hope that I will soon have the chance of introducing you to some of them. That is what I mean by the bright blue patches in the dark sky."

"Yes, I understand. But do you think that all that happens on its own."

"Of course I don't. Basically, there are two kinds of old age. One is old age of the body. That is the result of time and no one can escape it. The other is old age of the mind. Or rather, moral old age. To some extent it depends on the first, but it is also directly connected with the will. In a way, you only really become old if you consent to it. Just as the public health service and our own care and exercise can delay physical old age or at least make it bearable, we can also, I think, by a constant effort of the will, slow down—sometimes to the very last moment—old age of the soul. So there is no contradiction between accepting old age and staying young in spite of everything!"

A Song at Dawn for Géronte

Géronte, my dear old friend, you are trying so hard, and you are distressing me. You are flapping about like one of those winged insects that wants to fly through a pane of glass. They go up and down, but cannot get through. They make a rush and just hit the cold, thin wall of glass. They fall, stay for a moment dazed, then begin again, noisily flapping and beating their heads, but it is all in vain. I feel so sorry for them that I have to open the window and let them go free.

So, my dear friend, you are flapping and beating against old age that is just beginning—or rather has already begun. You don't want to think about it. You want to ignore it, yet again and again you come up against the solid reality of your age.

You refuse to give up any of your responsibilities and to cut back on any of your work. I get the impression that it gives you great pleasure to take on more and more. But the inevitable result is that you don't succeed. You make a mess of all the tasks that you pile up. You slow down what you hope to speed up. Because your mind is still clear, you are vaguely aware of it and it is transformed into bad humor that you get rid of on those near and dear to you.

It is very paradoxical, isn't it, that at the very time when you need to rest more, you go on holiday less than when you were in form. It is as though you are afraid that, if you go away, you won't find your place again when you come back.

Your health is suffering because of it, of course, and you are making up for it by taking a great number of drugs, stimulants, and tranquillizers. Your doctor has lavished good advice on you. You listen to it, but you only follow it in your imagination, and as soon as he has finished speaking, you just ask him for more miraculous drugs. Your wife is quite frightened and has often protested, but long ago you learned how to oppose her with passive resistance. You are never violent, but you are always victorious.

That doesn't prevent you from complaining a good deal at the risk of boring your listeners. You are overworked. You can't find anyone to help you. You have pains in your joints and your liver troubles you. And the stress.... Listening to you, I can't help thinking of the old comic song:

> "My liver's not right
> and my spleen is enlarged...."

and so on.

But despite all these troubles, you can still delude yourself into thinking you are young and, what is more, young enough to make the ladies' hearts beat more quickly. At a distance, it is true, you can still pass as young. But close up... ! Sometimes, when I see you, I think that you have suddenly got old.

Well, old friend (now is the time, if ever, to call you old), you ought to take time into account at last. Or, to speak even more openly, to listen to reason. Reason should tell you that you are no longer twenty, or even forty. You have even passed the difficult age of sixty.

If you had to go on working in order to stay alive, I would understand why you are so restless and agitated. But you have a nice little house, nothing lavish of course, but enough to keep you in comfort. Your children are all settled and married. If you can't rest completely—I hardly think you are capable of it—you can at least live without haste and overwork. You can enjoy some of the little pleasures that you have so far never had the time to enjoy. Your wife can share in them with you. You can take an interest in your grandchildren. And you can pray quietly and calmly to God.

That would be an act of kindness to yourself, Géronte, to accept your old age. If you don't, it will come crashing down on you suddenly, without warning, and you will be a wreck. Or else death will wring your neck just when you are least expecting it.

It is useless to think that it is not this kind of grace that your old (!) friend wants you to receive.

Serenade to Tircis

"Tircis, you must think of retiring." Every time I see you, Tircis, I am reminded of those sad words of Racan's. Yes, there is truth in the words of that old song—truth for you. It is time that you thought of retiring from active service.

You make me think of those old pieces of furniture that manage to survive somehow—repaired, propped up and painted over. You are not made up or even painted. You are illuminated like a medieval miniature. Your face is like the sunset over the ruins at Palmyra. You tint your hair the most unexpected colors. You wear the miniest of miniskirts that show your legs like two dry, twisted vines. You affect the manners of a young woman and simper so much that young women, who are aware of their superiority, only smile cruelly behind your back.

I knew you when we were both young together, Tircis. You were certainly not beautiful, but you were pretty, nice, and pleasant, like a little mossrose, but, as they say in the country districts, every rose becomes a rose-hip and runs to seed. And you long ago passed the age of being a rose—even an autumn rose. But either you don't know or you don't want to know. You cling to the appearance of youth, but youth has left you, so you wear the garment of youth. But soon the cloth will tear and fray and all that will be left in your hands is a thin, colorless rag.

It is a pity, because you could be what used to be called, not very politely I admit, a fine old woman. Your features are still good and you carry yourself well. You could crown your head with beautiful white hair and I certainly would not want to prevent you from having it waved—one of those waves that are called permanent but need to be renewed from time to time.

In the last century, ladies used to dress uniformly after about the age of fifty or so. The style of those dowagers was austere, imposing, and splendid. The color was almost always jet black and on their heads they wore bonnets like an old-fashioned beehive.

I would not dream of asking you to dress up like that, especially as women do not want to appear older now when they are middle-aged, but prefer to extend their youth endlessly. All that I would ask of you is to take account of your real age and to dress and behave in accordance with the date on your birth certificate. Make use of all that the beauty care industry can offer you, but don't misuse it. You may find it a bit difficult at first, but when you get used to it, you will feel all the better for it. You are a grandmother, Tircis! Why not think of those grandchildren you love so much? Be a real grandmother for them—a noble and dignified old woman, not a ridiculous one.

You are growing old badly. Try to grow old well, like fruit that ripens slowly until the day when it is ready to be picked. The apple blossom is beautiful in the spring and the full, red apple is beautiful at the end of autumn. Once it has been picked and put in the store-room, it remains perfect until the beginning of the next spring, when the apple trees are in blossom again.

Well, Tircis, I shall then be able to look at you without any reservations and without hiding a smile, and we shall be able to recall together our youth and how pretty you were. Who knows? I may even have been a little in love with you then.

Fine Days

It seems to you as though they were only yesterday, your fine days,
but long years separate you from them.
Now it is winter.
The days are short, though still too long.
The skies are grey and body and heart are cold.
The weight of your sorrows has bent you down
and grief has ploughed furrows in your face.
Don't cry, grandmother, don't believe that is the end of everything!
The sun is not dead.
There will be more fine days.

There will always be fine days
for those who have beauty in their hearts,
for those who have the sun in their souls.
There will always be fine days in time
until that fine day which will never end.

Growing Old Beautifully

If you actively accept old age and still remain young, you will grow old beautifully. Maybe you are thinking once again: He is speaking in paradoxes. Surely old age is by definition unsightly? Does it not make each one of us into a caricature of our former self? It deepens the lines both in our face and in our character. It is like a painter overemphasizing the features of his model on the preliminary outline of his portrait. How many real caricatures there are in the portrait gallery of old men! And old people are presented as no more attractive in literature. Think of the old misers—Harpagon in Molière's play and Balzac's Père Grandet—and the pitiful, ruined old rakes in the Don Juan tradition. Or just think of all those old people you have known whose eyes are dull and whose spirit is extinguished.

I think of them, believe me. I can still recall a terrible caricature drawn by Abel Faivre of an old lady stripped naked in front of the doctor, wearing only her hat. In the caption, the doctor is complaining: "I only wanted to examine your head, madam. It would have been quite enough to take off your hat!" And then there are those frightful old witches painted by Goya, the tips of their noses almost joining their pointed chins and their eyes flashing the fires of hell.

These pictures can, of course, be contrasted with others that are equally true to life and perhaps more so—those of really fine old men and women. Those majestic old bedouins of the North African desert, dressed in rags, but with the dignity of patriarchs! And the simple, but striking beauty of old French peasant men and women in my youth! In painting, of course, we have the classic examples of Old Testament figures in Rembrandt's presentation of old people emerging from the light and shade. And we have all met ordinary, insignificant men and women in our own lives on whom old age has conferred a surprising dignity.

When we were little children, did we think grandfather and grandmother were, to use the word we may have used then, "nasty"? Surely not! They loved us and we loved them and that love lit up their wrinkled old faces for us.

Victor Hugo once said that young men are handsome, but old men are great. It is not really as simple as that. There are some very unattractive young men—and young women. And there are some poor little old men and women who are certainly not great, but are no less attractive because of it.

After all, beauty—and that is what we are talking about here—is a complex and living reality that is born of a harmony between the body and the soul. A beautiful statue is only a statue and its beauty is purely formal. Living beauty, however, sometimes breathes through faces that are entirely lacking in classical harmony and physical perfection. I am thinking especially here of a little painting by Ghirlandajo of a child and an old man. The child is fair, fresh and angelic and the old man has a wrinkled, blotchy face and a red pimply nose, the sign of someone who was fond of a glass of wine. But there is in that old face such a clear reflection of love that it is made beautiful and ends by being very similar to the child's face.

A fine old man does not necessarily call God the Father to

mind—however we may imagine God the Father to be—or the four great prophets around the well at Dijon carved by Claus Sluter. Nor does a beautiful old lady necessarily have the bearing and the stature of a queen in exile. A very ordinary little old man can become a fine old man when his face is lit up by a smile. An unimportant old woman can rediscover the beauty of her younger days when she bends over the cradle containing her grandchild. In both these cases, the beauty is not the Devil's, but the beauty of God himself. And then those reclining figures on ancient tombs in our churches—death has made their stone features rigid, but has also given them a solemn harmony. Growing old beautifully is growing old in harmony between the body and the soul, in hope and peace.

This success at the end of one's days is not achieved automatically. We are not fashioned more by old age than we are by life itself. We make our life, and we make our old age or rather, we make a good deal of them and have to take into account everything outside us that cannot be controlled by our will. Should I also add here that we make our death?

The beauty of our body is maintained by good health, exercise, and care. It requires a constant effort. The same applies to beauty of every kind. If we let ourselves go, we go to the Devil. Together we shall see how much effort we have to make to grow old beautifully.

The Holy Spirit and Old Age

For us, who are Christ's brothers, growing old beautifully is growing old in Christ, in the overwhelming beauty of that God whose beauty is only dimly reflected in the beauty of the world.

The Holy Spirit was sent by that Christ and his presence in our hearts enables us to call God our Father. He speaks to us in our hearts, but he also speaks to us through Scripture, which is his work. Let us, therefore, listen to the Bible.

* * *

The extreme shortness of human life is lamented throughout the Old Testament and especially in the Psalms, the Book of Job and in the Wisdom literature. It is counted up quickly by the Old Testament authors: sixty or seventy years. Our lives pass like the wind or like a shadow. We are like those plants that flower in the morning and then wither away in the evening and are thrown on the fire. Even the just man, who is like a fine tree on the bank of the river, heavy with flowers and fruit, lasts only a short time—less than a tree.

It is not difficult to understand, then, in these conditions, that old age is seen in the Old Testament as a gift of God's grace and a precious reward. The person who wants to live for a long time will therefore honor his father and his mother and God will reward him with a happy old age, when he will see his children, his grandchildren, and even his great grandchildren. He will be like those great patriarchs, the ancestors of the people of God—Abraham, Isaac, and Jacob. Their great longevity is recorded in the book of Genesis.

Psalm 71 (17-24) is a cry of trust and hope and in it this teaching is summarized:

O God, from my youth thou hast taught me
  And I still proclaim thy wondrous deeds.
So even to old age and grey hairs,
  O God, do not forsake me,
till I proclaim thy might
  to all generations to come.
Thy power and thy righteousness, O God,
  reach the high heavens.

Thou who hast done great things,
  O God, who is like thee?
Thou who hast made me see many sore troubles
  wilt revive me again;
from the depths of the earth,
  thou wilt bring me up again.
Thou wilt increase my honor
  and comfort me again.

I will also praise thee with the harp
  for thy faithfulness, O my God.
I will sing praises to thee with the lyre,
  O holy one of Israel.
My lips will shout for joy,
  when I sing praises to thee;
my soul also, which thou hast rescued.

And my tongue will talk of thy righteous help all day long,
for they have been put to shame and disgraced
who sought to do me hurt.

* * *

Let us pause for a moment and look at a few of the great old men, patriarchs, or prophets, who figure in the Old Testament story.

First of all, there is Abraham, the father of the people and our father in faith. He was a pilgrim and a believer. Followed by his caravan, he looked for the Lord along many ways and finally encountered him under the oak trees at Mambre. He loved his wife Sarah tenderly but had no descendants to continue their line and had to resort to adoption, so he thought. They had reached the age when they could no longer hope for children of their own, but the Lord spoke to him through the voice of his messengers, telling him that he would beget posterity more numerous than the stars in the sky.

Abraham believed in the Lord's word—quite simply believed. And the Lord's promise was fulfilled. Then the Lord spoke again, claiming the sacrifice of Isaac, Abraham's only child. Once again, Abraham did not hesitate. He listened and obeyed. The Lord rewarded him and spared Isaac, thus confirming his promise.

Saint Paul saw Abraham as the outstanding example of faith that justifies man. For us, his spiritual descendants, he recalls the fact that faith is not connected with age and that it makes us ready to remain in God's will, even when he asks us to give those who are most dear to us. Abraham also shows us, by his example, that our pilgrimage will last until the end of our life. Lord, I will walk, like Abraham, until I die, in search of your face.

In his youth, Jacob was a cunning fellow who tricked his

brother Esau of his birthright and his father's blessing. He was the ancestor of all cunning individuals. But he was also a strong man who struggled all night with the angel and was beaten only in the early hours of the morning, when his opponent used his strength to dislocate Jacob's thigh. He became Israel and was even able to prevail against God.

In his old age, his malice and his strength both disappeared and all that was left was a gentle heart and a father's love. He loved and mourned for his son Joseph. He loved and mourned for his son Benjamin. He loved and mourned for them so much that, in the end, God weakened and gave them both back to him. Israel was able to prevail against God again, but this time by his love and his tears. We shall love like Jacob and, like him, we shall let our hearts melt in love.

Moses, powerful and solitary, was not a patriarch, but a prophet speaking in God's name and a leader taking his motley stiff-necked flock of Hebrews through the wilderness, that mass of strolling flesh looking back with regret at the fleshpots of Egypt. He had both experience and authority. He did not see God face to face, since he would have died if he had, but he caught a glimpse of his shadow and spoke to him in the lofty lonely place where thunder and lightning reigned. He gave his people laws and led them to the promised land.

He did not tread himself on that promised land. In expiation of his sins, he was only able to see it from afar, just before he died, from the summit of Mount Nebo. It was a country flowing with living water, milk, and honey. That excellent Black American film, *Green Pastures,* showed us the aged Moses, sitting on the mountain, resting while he was waiting for death and looking at the promised land. The Hebrews were filing past him, each one of them tenderly putting a hand on his shoulder.

Like Moses, we shall walk on. We shall work and struggle

without looking for a reward for ourselves. We shall prepare for those who follow us a promised land and better times. Our reward will be, as Henri de Tourville once said, that we have made the path more beautiful for those who will come after us.

* * *

Apart from a few passages in the Epistles, there is little about old age in the New Testament, and human wickedness did not leave Christ any time to grow old himself, in order to provide us with a model. There are, however, several old men and women in the Gospels. They are less obtrusive than the Old Testament patriarchs and prophets, but also less severe.

When Joseph and Mary went to offer the infant Jesus at the Temple in Jerusalem, they met two old people there—Simeon and the prophetess Anna. These were simple, humble, and God-fearing people who lived in that great building full of cells, which was the Temple of Herod, so that they could be closer to the Lord and spend their days and nights there in prayer. They were waiting for the salvation of Israel. As soon as they saw Jesus, they no longer hesitated. They, with their purity of vision, at once recognized him. Inspired, Simeon took the child in his arms and sang the canticle that is still sung at compline by the Church as an evening prayer:

> Lord, now lettest thou thy servant depart in peace,
> according to thy word,
> for my eyes have seen thy salvation.

My eyes have seen your light—I have lived long enough and I can now without fear confront the shadows of death. The song that comes from my lips proclaims both your faithfulness and the fulfillment of my life. A beautiful old Latin antiphon, sung at the feast of Candlemass, tells us that the old man carried the child and the child led the old man. That antiphon defines

Christian old age very well. We carry Christ in our spirit, heart, and hands and he guides and directs us. And when our life is fulfilled, we have the right to sing: "I am ready now, Lord. Let your servant depart in peace." Let your servant go toward that last encounter between time and eternity.

Then there is Saint Joseph. He is traditionally depicted as a fine old man with as magnificent a beard as Charlemagne's, although we ought to note in passing that the emperor had no beard! This picture of Saint Joseph is probably wrong. It was the custom for Jews to marry at about the age of thirty. When Joseph married Mary, he, therefore, must have been in the prime of life. But he got old like everyone else and in all probability died in Nazareth before Jesus began to spread the good news. He breathed his last between the God-Man and the Virgin Mary, who helped him to cross the threshold between life and death. And what a death!

It is hardly surprising that, at a time when Christians liked to contemplate death—perhaps a little too much and to the detriment of their contemplation of life—they chose Joseph as the patron saint of the good death. Why, then, should we not do the same? We old people are, after all, forced, whether we want to or not, by our age to meditate about what used to be called the last things. When I was very young, I was taught to recite a little prayer: "Jesus, Mary, and Joseph help me in my last agony. Jesus, Mary, and Joseph, let me die in your dear and holy company." I was much too young, of course, to understand what I was praying, but now I can understand the words well enough and they come back to me again and again.

And what about the Virgin Mary? We always think of her as young, as she was when she received the message from the archangel Gabriel. As the archetype of woman, virgin, and mother, she is always and eternally young, but in the course of her human history she certainly became old. This happened when she was living at Ephesus in the house of John, the disciple whom Jesus loved and to whom he had entrusted her when he was hanging on the cross. She must have kept house for John, because it is hardly possible to imagine her inactive, but at the same time she reflected about everything that she had, in Saint Luke's words, kept in her heart—everything, in other words, that is contained in the mysteries of the rosary and depicted by the Flemish painter. Then she fell asleep in Christ, waiting for him to fetch her for her assumption into heaven. The feast of the falling asleep of the Virgin is a popular one in the Eastern Church. Many women live longer than the husbands whom they have loved and even than their sons and the idea of the Virgin in old age may be a model for them.

Finally, we should not forget John the Evangelist, whom we have already mentioned. In the Gospels, we see him as a young man, probably the youngest and the purest of all the apostles. He was also one of the most fiery—a real son of the thunder, as Christ called him. According to a very credible tradition, he narrowly escaped martyrdom, went into exile, became very old and wrote his Gospel and the epistles in his old age as a meditation on the Word of life whom he had known in his youth. At the end of his life, it is said that he repeated again and again the words that sum up the whole spirit of his work: "My little children, love one another."

Those are beautiful words for an old man who had worked so hard and experienced so much! May they be always on the lips of every Christian old person! . . . I have experienced, suffered, and struggled and only one great lesson seems to be important: "My little children, love one another!"

Men and Women Like Us

Do you think you are encouraging us? You are rather putting us off! Your examples are all too far off and too exalted. Patriarchs, heroes, and saints! How can we poor old people model ourselves on such figures?

Be patient and trust me. I have already shown you two sunny portraits—faded, but still very much alive, taken from my family album. To prove to you that it is possible to grow old beautifully, I would like now to introduce you to some fine old people, men and women like us, perhaps a bit better than us and close enough to us not to put us off, but sufficiently far above us to invite us to aim higher.

The first is Father Louis Cousin. We called him "Father," but he was really a lay religious and belonged to the Marianists. The title "Father" suited him well, though, because he was a fatherly, even a patriarchal celibate and this made it possible for us to respect him and to trust him at the same time. I met him at the end of his life. He was a fine old man, erect, alert, and dignified, with a big white beard and clear, pure eyes. He had been the Sillonists' spiritual director and perhaps, if they had listened more attentively to him, they would have avoided the painful misfortunes that befell their movement. He preserved, from this long period of working together with young people, an easy way of making contact with them. Even when he was very old, he could without difficulty listen to them, understand them, and love them.

At the time when the movement known as the Companions of Saint Francis was being founded, I was also a rebellious youth and, although we did not set fire to cars, we were in other ways just as violent in our self-expression as young people today. I threw all old men on to the rubbish-heap of history, certainly if they seemed to be behind the times. But even then, young and impatient though I was, I got on easily with that old man. He did not embarrass me in any way or make me feel uncomfortable and restless! He was so serene that he seemed no longer to be part of time. He gave the impression of being in touch with eternity. He was ageless.

Henri Colas, the singer, was twenty years older than I and he too was a member of the Sillon movement. Although there was such a difference between us in years, he became one of my closest friends. He soon spotted my gift for writing songs and singing and was not at all jealous professionally, but at once asked me to join him in his apostolate of the song. He published my work in a review that he edited and gave me a great deal of help and advice when it came to making my first records.

All the same, we were quite different from each other and our songs were also different. Each of us was marked by his generation. He was in the tradition of Pierre Dupont and Théodore Botrel, and I was strongly influenced by folklore. When I first knew him, he was resplendent in the brilliance of his mature years, but I watched him grow gradually older until he reached the point where he could no longer continue the demanding work of a wandering singer. Eventually he had to give up being God's tramp.

Although he had sung for three generations, the last generation of young people forgot him in favor of new and younger spirits, who many of whom lacked his talent, I am afraid. Then he lost his beloved wife. He had led a wandering, generous life and had put hardly anything in store for the winter, but, although life was difficult in his old age, he did not lose any of the joy that had always been with him in his earlier years. He retired to a little house at Guillerval on the River Juisne, in the wide open country of corn fields between Paris and Orléans, and at once began to take care of the spiritual life of the village, almost replacing the parish priest and gathering a wide circle of young people around him. He was the living center of a great network of friendships in the region.

The Great Friend, whose praises he had so often sung in the past, continued to pour rare and precious graces on him. He still had the outline of a young man and the heart of a twenty year old, and he kept to the very end of his life an astonishing ability to attract young people. It was wonderful to see him, when he was almost eighty, surrounded by young men and women. He had the wisdom of an old man and the gaiety of a young one. One of his greatest sorrows was that he had never had children of his own, but the Lord gave him, who was one of his best servants, numerous spiritual offspring. He died happily and peacefully.

My friend Ernest Lancelot, who was also a faithful follower of Henri Colas, had fourteen children. He had the good fortune not to lose a single one and he led them all on the right way and some of them reached great heights. Like his fellow townsman from Orléans, Charles Péguy, he accepted, together with his admirable wife Isabelle, the great adventure of bringing up a large family in the modern world. He saw that adventure as a pilgrimage, and he was, of course, a devoted Companion of Saint Francis. His family responsibilities were sometimes overwhelming, but they did not prevent him from militant social and political action and he was one of the pioneers of the Christian family movement in France. I have seldom met in any man such a balanced mixture of common sense and calm audacity.

When his greatly loved wife passed over from time into eternity, he withdrew from activity and waited in silence and prayer for the moment when he would rejoin her. He did not, however, withdraw into himself and, in constant contact with the Church and the world, he was overjoyed by the Second Vatican Council. He died surrounded by his children and grandchildren—a true Biblical patriarch.

Mother Saint-Pierre belonged to an order of nuns which did excellent work that was for the most part unknown. She worked hard all her life, which was very long, and gave a great deal of herself, with all the simplicity of a peasant woman from the French Alps, for that is what she continued to be, despite her religious habit. Toward the end of her life, she had nothing more to give but her goodness, wisdom, and almost unceasing prayer, visible in the rosary that was almost always in her hands.

I loved to talk to her about everything and nothing—both in the everything and the nothing of her conversation, God was present. Once, when we were talking about my vocation, she had an insight which could only have been the product of a deep spiritual understanding. She was very frightened, I remember, when death first beckoned her as a very old woman. That should not surprise anyone. The most holy people of all are sometimes most deeply afraid of death. This is partly because their holiness is inseparably connected with a great natural vitality which instinctively shies away from the inevitable end of life. It is also because such people are unhappy when they see themselves, at the end, in the terrible light of God. But they accept—as Mother Saint-Pierre accepted—and die peacefully.

I have invented none of this, nor have I indulged in romance or hagiography. I have simply reported what I have seen and I have spoken of people I knew. Well, as Saint Augustine said after his conversion, what others have done, why should not I? And why should not we?

There Will Be More Fine Days

I can hear you, young woman, singing that old song:

"How short the fine days are!"

You really don't believe these words and you are right not to.
The fine days are short, however, and they pass by more quickly than the clouds pass across the moon when the wind is blowing.
Experience will teach you that they last no longer than the colors of the rainbow.
For every sunny day, how many bad days there are—and how many are grey!
But, young woman, even if sorrow strikes you and death surrounds you,
don't believe that is the end of everything!
Stand up again and smile, the sun is not dead.
There will be more fine days.

I can hear you, unhappy mother, grieving for the fine days of your youth:

"How short the fine days are!"

Anxieties, suffering and prayers have etched lines on your face
and each of your wrinkles is a scar.
Each of your white hairs is a mark.
The bitter winds have blown away your illusions like dead leaves.
Autumn is close with its mists and cold rain.
But don't believe that is the end of everything!
Stand up again and smile, the sun is not dead.
There will be more fine days.

I can hear you, grandmother, singing in a thin, piping voice, like the sound of a musical box, the song of your youth:

"How short the fine days are!"

Call Me Back, Lord

Lord, you created life and overcame death.
Lord, you create and know
our days, our hours and our destinies—
you are the Lord of time.
You can call me back now into your peace.
I have seen your light
and that is enough for me.
Call me back, Lord.

I have lived the life, Lord, that you gave me.
I have learnt, loved, suffered, and fought.
I have tried, by my reason, to understand the world,
from one clear light to the next,
from mystery to mystery,
but now I have come to the end of the unfathomable mystery
where light and darkness mingle.
Call me back, Lord.

I have experienced fully all that a man can experience—
in the power and purity of youth,
in the balance of maturer years,

in the gentle and weakening light of old age.
I have drunk the full cup of life
and have celebrated life with my song.

Thank you for all these gifts, Lord.
What have I still to expect?
What new scent? What new color?
Call me back, Lord.

I have loved, Lord, with the heart that you put in my breast.
I have known love and friendship.
But those whom you gave me to love—
you have taken them back into your eternity.
No doubt I am still able to love,
but it is not quite the same love,
that fresh, new love of springtime.
I can feel the time coming when I shall no longer have the strength to love.
Call me back, Lord.

I have suffered, Lord, because we have to suffer to be human.
I have suffered in my body and my soul.
I have carried my cross on difficult climbs.
I am not bargaining with you about my suffering, Lord,
any more than your Son bargained about his,
but I am afraid—
I draw back from that moment
when, on the way of the cross,
I may fall without being able to get up again
because I can go no further
and will not have the courage to go as far as Calvary.
Call me back, Lord.

Call Me Back, Lord

I have struggled, Lord, and fought
for you and for my brothers
and I bear the scars that I have received in the battle.
But I am afraid of the time
when I shall no longer be able to fight
and no longer be able, like Moses, to stretch out my arms on the high place
while others fight on the plain.
Call me back, Lord.

I have learnt, Lord, that all life is waiting
waiting for your Light.
All life is climbing—
climbing up to Love.
I have waited—this is the hour of meeting.
I have climbed and stumbled—now I feel the wind at the top.

Call me back, Lord.

It Is Time to Retire . . .

We have decided to accept old age. Let us consider the practical consequences of this decision. The first is—retirement.

During the Second Empire of France, when Hortense Schneider and Thérésa were singing about the hussars of the Imperial Guard, the garrisons stationed in small French towns organized torchlight retreats with the aim of inspiring the citizens with feelings of heroism. These took place on Sunday evenings and a little refrain was often sung to a trumpet tune. It began with these words:

> It is time to retire!
> Trooper, back to your quarters!

This little song still has a very topical interest. I am not thinking here just of an army retiring, but of retirement in general. It is a subject that always provokes those who face it to discussion.

Most of us can be divided into certain categories. Some of us are right-wing, others are on the left. But it goes further than this. There are those who always want the windows shut and those who want them open. There are those of us who are best in the morning and those who come to life at night. Some people like dogs and others prefer cats. And then—and here I come to the point—certain people want to retire from work as soon as they can, whereas others want to put it off to the latest possible date.

Both those who want early retirement and those who want to retire late have excellent reasons for their preference. Not all of them, of course, are based purely on reason. Circumstances and personal taste play an important part.

I shall not try to settle this dispute, as it is not my aim in this book to deal with social questions. I will just limit myself to a few matters of ordinary common sense. It is obvious that a man whose work is thankless, tiring, dangerous, or simply uninteresting should want to retire at the earliest possible moment. In his place, we would all do the same. At the same time, it is equally normal that a man who finds his work absorbing should not want to retire. The idea that retirement should fall like a guillotine on everyone at a certain age is pretty inhuman.

Retirement pensions ought clearly to allow those who draw them to live in dignity, and that means at least enough to live on. It is not exactly an ideal form of retirement to be cooped up along with other old people in an old people's home. This practice must have been first introduced at the beginning of industrial society, with its great contrast between wealth and dire poverty. Now, however, it is out of date and unjust. If an old person wants or has to go into an old people's home, he ought to be able to spend his days there in a way in which he will be able to preserve both his freedom and his dignity.

We are, after all, pretty wide of the mark! And how many people I have known, including my own father, who worked to the last day of his life, simply because they hadn't the means to retire! Yet now, in our prosperous society, retirement is regarded as a right. We believe, because we have contributed to the wealth of the community by our work, that the community has to repay us when we are no longer working by letting us spend our old age in peace, protected from need and suffering. The society that we have helped to create is so overflowing with good things that it does not know what to do with them. Our conviction, moreover, is so strong that we think that it is in a state of serious disorder if it does not reward us in this way when we are old.

But we old people also have a social duty to retire, not only because we have to make way for the young people who are coming up and have a right to live, but also because it would be unreasonable for us to cling on to positions and functions which we can no longer carry out properly because of our declining strength. When I was young, I used to hate the way the Third Republic of France seemed to be dominated in every sphere by old men. I have not changed my mind since I have grown old. "Woe to the city whose prince is a youth!" Scripture declares, but I would say: Woe to the society whose old men have all the power to make decisions.

In farming, there was a good practice known as the rotation of crops. In society too, there ought to be a rotation of ages. If there are to be exceptions to this, they would only be a confirmation of the rule.

Those in authority in society always think that they are indispensable and irreplaceable. This may be true in a number of cases, but for the most part it is a great illusion. Or it might be more correct to call it a partial mistake. One strong personality can never completely replace another strong personality, simply because of their differences. The one who is retiring will not find a successor who will continue his work in exactly the same way. He will have to make the most of discontinuity in continuity.

The old man carries on! There is something very sad about

this kind of announcement. When an old man carries on too long in his position of power, persistently exercising authority because he is convinced that he cannot be replaced, he always risks spoiling and even in fact spoils what he holds most dear. How many businesses and industries have been ruined because some terrible old grandfather has not been able to let go of power in time? Sometimes they have even died "in harness" without trying to find a successor. Some of these terrible old rulers of modern empires have even refused to believe that they would ever die! How many movements have been brought to a final standstill by their founders, who were just not able to hand the torch on to the next man! One great old man, Georges Clemenceau, said: "The cemeteries are full of irreplaceable old men."

All these ideas are very reasonable and right, however general they may be, but where, you will ask, are they leading us? We need more precise details. For example, at what age should we retire?

I am afraid I cannot answer that question. Everything depends on the individual, his personality, and his job. I can only give a piece of wise advice: You have to go, however much those around you may regret your going and however little they want to throw you out. It is much better for your departure to be regretted than for you to be propped up.

Let me illustrate this by a true story. An old friend of mine, a devoted and holy parish priest, was beginning to feel his powers failing. He decided to retire from the parish and told the parishioners of this decision. There was at once a chorus of sorrowful, pleading and protesting voices: Oh, don't do that to us, Father! Don't leave us in the lurch! We need you! Please stay on with us!

They all caught hold of the skirts of his soutane (the garment was still worm in those days) and hung on with all their might. My old friend was very touched and gave way to their entreaties. He was wrong. Ten years later, the whole parish was clamoring for him to go. But this time, entrenched in senile stubbornness, he refused to go.

What is the moral of this story? It is this. Once you have decided, after deep reflection, to retire from your work, do not be held back. The day will come when those who pleaded with you to stay will find every way of getting rid of you.

If you are free to choose yourself, retire as soon as your work begins to weigh you down, as soon as you are conscious of doing it as a habitual task, a routine, as soon as you no longer feel up to it and as soon as you begin to fear change in it. These are not amusing observations? The unlucky Gil Blas, Le Sage's hero, learned this to his misfortune when, following the instructions of his boss, the archbishop, he warned him that his last sermon had a touch of apoplexy in it. The archbishop did not react in a very friendly way, and Gil Blas lost his job as his secretary. But, however painful some observations may be, it is better to make them oneself, before everyone else makes them.

You should also choose the moment to retire so that you have the leisure to benefit from your retirement. What is the use of retiring if you cannot enjoy the freedom that it brings you—if, in other words, your mind is no more than an empty space and your body just a collection of broken down museum pieces? We do not, as they used to think, live in order to work. We work to live! If the cap fits, wear it!

Do We Have To Get Out of Harness?

Do we have to get out of harness? After all that I have said about retiring, this question may seem to be less important, even unnecessary. But I don't think it is.

Retirement and getting out of harness are not exactly the same. When we retire, we give up a professional responsibility. We no longer do a certain kind of regular work that we are obliged to do. We go back—literally retire—in order to be free to leap forward without being encumbered by the tasks we did before. This does not mean that we give up all our professional activities or all activities of any kind. Getting out of harness, on the other hand, is giving up every kind of active service. When you take off a horse's harness, you take him out of the shafts and away from his work of drawing the carriage. He goes back back to the stable to spend the remainder of his days resting, eating, sleeping, and dreaming the sort of dreams that horses have.

At the turn of the century, retirement, which was the privilege of a few people, meant getting out of harness completely. The most strenuous activities indulged in by retired people were fishing, playing cards, and drinking an apéritif before meals. More enterprising souls went in for a little gardening. Ladies in retirement practiced three sports which were considered eminently suitable for their sex—sweeping, knitting, and backbiting. Those of a pious disposition helped to decorate the altar of the parish church with natural or artificial flowers. They lived rather like old nags whose harness had been removed for the last time and who had been turned out on to the grass of the fields to vegetate.

This ideal kind of retirement has not disappeared completely from our society, but now that so many more people can look forward to retirement, it is no longer so widespread. Many retired people want to combine rest with activity and lead what is known as an active retirement. Some people try to supplement their pension by doing work on the side and even accept lower rates for the jobs they do. It is not a very sociable thing to do. Undercutting, the economists call it, in competition with workers in full-time employment who cost more.

Opinions are divided, obviously. If you are able to give up work, give it up and relax, some say. Others insist: Stay in harness! One hale and hearty old doctor wrote a book some years ago with the title: "Don't get out of harness! What would you do if you did?"

There is clearly no general rule to be applied. Attitudes vary according to the person and his age. There are old people who only have the strength to rest—as Jacques Brel sang so sadly in his popular song years ago: "From bed to armchair—from armchair to bed!" Other old people remain lively and alert until they are unbelievably old. Some have exhausted their activities in earlier life and can find no more to do. Others cannot tear themselves away from their work, like those old railway workers who used to plant their cabbages only a stone's throw from a station when they retired so that they could hear the sound of the trains as they went past and—most important of all!—fill in for the station master when he was away. Like the poet Charles Cros, they believed that "happiness may only be found in railway stations." But that is a matter of taste and opportunity.

There is, however, some advice that can be applied to everyone. In most cases, it would seem that it is much better to break away completely from the work that one has always done. At the same time, the break should not be sudden, since this often causes harm, but gradual. It is always very hard for those who have been in a position of leadership to see their place taken by others. They often find it very difficult to resist poking their noses in what is no longer their business. There are, of course, exceptions. Some are motivated by what Rabelais cabled a "dire lack of *pecunia*" and others by their membership of one of those professions that cling so persistently that it is impossible to get rid of it completely. One such profession—the one that I know personally—is journalism. In such circumstances, it may be necessary to become no more than an enlightened amateur or even a kind of ghost, haunting one's profession, one of those dead men who has to be killed off.

Rest should not be confused in retirement with idleness. Retirement, after all, gives us the right to be lazy. This is the right claimed by Paul Lafargue in a little spiritual tract which has so much in common with the famous proclamation by Karl Marx and which both capitalists and socialists would do well to study. But man can abuse this right as much as any other. If we make use of our retirement just to do nothing at all or simply to waste our time, then we shall condemn ourselves to boredom. We shall become stunted and even debased. In the past, the familiar figure of the man who retired early to live on his investments and found it hard to go out to collect his dividends when the weather was hot was not an admirable type of human being or a model of old age.

Rest is not exactly the same as inactivity. A long time ago, Lord Chesterfield told his son that a change of activity was a kind of rest. Some people want to be always on the move when they have retired, and so they deliberately misinterpret this saying. But we should not forget that the manual worker who spends his time doing odd jobs in retirement and the intellectual who reads avidly the books he has never been able to read are both resting.

What about women? The advice that I have given applies to those who have had a profession, but there are still many women who have just kept house and raised a family. They never retire. They always have a needle, a broom, or a ladle in their hands. There is a kind of retirement, of course, for mothers, when they finally accept the fact that their children have become responsible adults and do not need them as much as they did in the past. They retire when they accept themselves as grandmothers and do not want to weigh their grandchildren or their husband down with a surfeit of motherly sentiment that can become tyrannical or else resemble that of a broody hen.

We have a choice then. We can get out of harness or we can stay in harness. Either choice has its real problems. We have to get out of harness if we find that we lack the strength or the courage to go on pulling a certain carriage. But we also have to remain in harness and choose carriages that we can pull. We have to change carriages as some become too heavy for us. That is only wise.

Going on Living Until the End

But what carriage should we choose? How are we to fill in the empty hours of retirement? How can we spend our voluntary or enforced leisure?

Very many older people cannot answer these questions. Their work has filled the greater part of their lives. In mind and body they have been taken up by it and fashioned by it. They have become nothing but men of their profession or trade. As soon as they give it up, they languish and die like fish out of water. Apart from their work, they are drawn to nothing and cannot do anything. Work, travel, and sleep—the three elements of life. The first and most important is work. Travel just takes you to your work and from it. Work is also your colleagues. Away from work and your pals, all that is left is sleep, and that is very much like death.

If the statistics are correct, many men die within a year of retiring. Is this the result of accumulated fatigue? For a great number, it probably is, but it is also the result of boredom—for once, the phrase "bored to death" would seem to be true. A man retires and dies of boredom as much as of grief. He can only go on clinging to life if it provides him with an interest, an aim, and a meaning. When he gives up work, life loses all meaning. So he lets himself sink into the great sleep of death.

It is a simple fact of human experience that women are better able to endure old age and retirement than men. They have more biological vitality than men, of course. But they also have more to occupy them in their own sphere, the home. And as a rule, even when they have had professional employment or work outside the house, they have never been so completely oriented toward it.

In the past, many of the people who worked in the cities had come there from the country. When they retired, they often went back to their villages to spend their old age there. They frequently also went back to the jobs they had done when they were young.

Now, however, many such people stay in the cities where they have worked when they retire and, if they went back to the country, they would not know what to do there and would be as idle as they are in the suburbs of Paris or Lyon. Retirement to the country may soon be the privilege of rich people or at least of fairly well off families with a second home, a telephone, and a car.

I know of no more pitiful spectacle than that of old, unoccupied people whose life is one long yawn only broken by radio and television broadcasts. (And these often make them yawn even more.) I often have the impression that these men are no more than an extra piece of furniture in their little flats and houses, always in their wives' way. So much so, in fact, that they end by irritating their wives beyond measure and seek refuge in drinking in the local cafe, with all that that entails. The more the wives spread out in their homes, the more out of place their husbands feel when they do not know what to do there.

We should not anticipate death by becoming physically and spiritually immobile. Living is moving about, doing things and being creative. Old age and retirement should not be an anticipation of death—which will come quickly enough without our having to make an advance payment. We should go on living until the end.

The Important Flower Is the Rose

"Smoking his pipe and looking at his roses." Who was it who described the peak of happiness for the man living in the Loire valley with these words? I do not remember, but I gladly take it over and apply it to myself. It is really pleasant to smoke one's pipe and look at one's roses. It is wonderful to smell the sharp odor of tobacco mingling with the sweet scent of the flowers. I may be an ardent son of the Rhône valley, but on this point I feel very much at one with the people of the Loire valley.

But why smoking a *pipe*? Because it goes together with resting, relaxation, and calm meditation. Smoking while meditating or meditating while smoking—what does it matter? So long as our thoughts follow the coils of the smoke upwards. The inveterate smoker of cigarettes is, after all, a maniac—a toxicomaniac. The man who smokes a pipe is usually an epicure and a man of wisdom.

And why the *rose*? Surely other flowers would do just as well! In Holland it would be the tulip. Then there are so many flowers all with their special virtues—the lily, the iris, the gladiola, and even good middle-class solid flowers such as the begonia, the petunia, and the dahlia. But no, there is none to equal the rose, no other flower to match its classical shape, color, or perfume. The rose is the flower *par excellence*. As Gilbert Bécaud used to sing: "The important flower is the rose." And he was right.

The meeting between the very prosaic pipe and the highly poetic rose gives me great pleasure—a simple, healthy, and natural pleasure, one of those pleasures that God wanted men to have when he endowed them with senses.

I am sorry for those city-dwellers who hardly ever see a rose growing in splendor on a bush, but are only familiar with the flower when it is cut and doomed to death. I am sorry for women who are certainly able to savor the rose, but will never taste the pipe.

In my mind's eye, I can still see my grandfather sitting in the evening sun smoking, in the garden which he cultivated with such love. He smoked a carefully seasoned clay pipe—one of those pipes costing two or three pence in those days, no longer obtainable now, but then very well suited to the less than modest resources of those who smoked them. Sucking at his pipe, he would proudly contemplate his vegetables and flowers. He did not speak much and loved to be alone, sunk in thought. What were his thoughts? I never knew, and it is quite likely that he did not either. But his relaxed face showed that his soul was at peace. When I joined my childish thoughts to his old man's meditation, I was always careful not to disturb him. He did not stop gardening, smoking his pipe, and dreaming until he was seventy-seven, when he was struck down by a heart attack, like an oak tree struct by lightning. In fact, his solid, heavy body always reminded me of an oak tree, so perhaps his end was the right one.

"Smoking his pipe and looking at his roses." I hardly need to add that the pleasure is increased if you have planted the rose trees yourself and have cared so well for them that you have slowly made them capable, as the old song says, of "bearing a rose in the month of May." A certain kind of rest is also a form of activity—a gentle, quiet activity which does not stretch you, but keeps your mind and body in shape, as sportsmen say. Smoking your pipe and looking at your roses is one of those activities. I would say the same of that essentially feminine occupation—knitting. It took me a long time to understand why women had such a passion for manipulating long needles and threads of wool. I ended by realizing that knitting was for them what smoking a pipe was for men—a gentle mania, a way of making use of your energies by taking care of them, a task calling for a little attention and keeping your hands busy, but leaving your mind and your tongue free. And all this combined with the chance of breathing in the scent of roses!

I hope that the great urban explosion will leave us enough earth, between the factories and blocks of flats, and enough pure air for us to grow a few roses and make them bloom—just enough for us to look at them and smoke our pipes.

Compensations

One of the few advantages of old age and one of the undoubted benefits of retirement are that we can satisfy a few old and hitherto suppressed longings and indulge in a few fantasies that we could not allow ourselves to have during our working life. Old age and retirement have their compensations, then, because they give us back at least a little of the freedom that made our younger days so enchanting.

I have never been more aware of this than when I was a prisoner-of-war. Contrary to what those who have never been prisoners think, that "long vacation" was not a period of enforced idleness or interminable boredom going on until the moment of freedom came and spent behind barbed wire and watchtowers. After the first few weeks of disorientation and the growing conviction that it was going to last a long time, the prisoners were able to find ways of preventing time from hanging heavily on their hands. Universities were founded, choirs and dramatic societies were formed, and all kinds of groups and clubs were set up. In the end, we had so much to keep us busy that our diaries were soon filled up. I was struck and indeed, to use an old-fashioned word, very edified by the regular presence of so many older senior officers at our courses and talks. Not all of them, of course. For some of them, being a prisoner-of-war was one long game of bridge, barely interrupted by meals and sleep. But others were very strict in their attendance at our activities—so much so that many students would have reason to envy them. They would come with their stools and blankets, listen attentively, take notes and question the lecturer closely. They had a real thirst for knowledge and an appetite for culture that they had never been able to satisfy in their youth. At last, I recognized, they were fulfilled, catching up with all that they had missed in the past because of military duties if they were on the active list or professional work if they were on the reserve. Several told me that being a prisoner-of-war was the best time of their lives. They did then what they had always wanted to do.

If you want it to be, your old age could be such a time of compensation. That book that you have always wanted to read but has always remained unread because you never had the time—here it is! You can read it now. That film which attracted you so much, but which you never saw—you can perhaps see it now on the little screen. You often thought of going to a concert, but work, tiredness, or other duties prevented you from going. But now you are free and, if you are afraid to go to a concert hall, you can hear all the best orchestras in the world on your radio. Have you always wanted to go for long walks in the country? If you live in or near the fields, the whole of nature is calling to you now that you are retired. In Paris, you have all the museums, exhibitions, and lectures that you need. When I used to give talks on the Côte d'Azur, at Nice, or Cannes, at least a third of my audience consisted of retired people. Some had come, I know, just because they wanted to overcome their boredom—and I do not know whether I always succeeded in helping them to victory! But others came quite certainly in order to satisfy an intellectual curiosity about the subject (or perhaps a personal curiosity about the lecturer). Look around you. Dig deeply into your memory. You are bound to find some unsatisfied longings that go back a long way, perhaps even as far as your early childhood. Now you can satisfy them. Make really good use of the time that is still left to you!

These are no more than a few late compensations, you will say scornfully. A bit like those people who were poor but longed to be rich and eat Gargantuan meals when they were young and who have amassed wealth and possessions in adult life. Rolling in money, but suffering from permanent indigestion, they have in old age to put up with a diet of noddles and mineral water. You could not be entirely wrong if you thought that. If you go for a walk in the forest, you will not be doing it with the legs you had at twenty. If you go to the mountains, you will most of the time have to be content with looking at the peaks and the glaciers. If you open a book or listen to a record, neither will have all the freshness of a new experience for you. We have lived for a long time, my old friend, so we have lost our teeth, our hair, our illusions, and our innocence. And we shall lose even more. . . .

When you taste new wine at the age of seventy, is it less good because you are able to compare it with other wines? When you hear some Mozart that you do not know, is it less beautiful because you know other works by the same composer? If you are really to enjoy these things, you should not be blasé or indifferent to everything and you must have preserved a little youthfulness of spirit and a little corner in your heart reserved for joy. You should also thank Providence for allowing you to make up for all the opportunities you have missed and for compensating—however late—for all the losses of your younger days.

One final suggestion: Why not go back now and then to the authors who pleased you so much in the past? Jules Verne has, heaven knows why, become popular again, and there are many cheap editions of his works available now. I have enjoyed re-reading him. The impression I have of him now, in old age, only confirms the memories of my childhood and I have, what is more, made many new discoveries—things that escaped me when I was a boy. Some of you will have studied the French classics, but at an age when you were only able to understand half of what they were saying. (And if I give you half, I am being generous!) Why not arrange a meeting today with Corneille and Racine or with Pascal and Bossuet? A long time ago, it was claimed that retired judges, with their early education in classical civilization, spent their leisure time reading Horace, and I certainly knew two old priests who used to read Homer in Greek. But, even if we did learn Latin and Greek at school, most of us don't know them any more—with a few honorable exceptions, of course. I would suggest that you just go back, with all your experience of life and your much more refined taste, to the fables of La Fontaine which you used to recite like parrots when you were kids at school. And then read those that your teachers didn't show you. You will be pleased and astonished by the experience, I can assure you.

Going back in this way to the past is not just a question of being compensated. It is a way of finding fulfillment.

Hobbies

What is a hobby? It is a secondary occupation to which you can usually devote only part of your time, but which you follow with great pleasure and passion. It is not your professional work, even though it may well involve some hard work and difficulty. Nor is it a game—playing bridge, whist, or poker, often for money, is certainly not a hobby. A man may have a mania for his hobby, but his hobby is not a mania. Smoking, chewing tobacco, or taking snuff may well be manias, but they are not hobbies. I would define some hobbies as the amateur practice of what is for others professional work. So gardening, doing odd jobs, Sunday painting, and good old-fashioned fishing are all hobbies.

Scouting used to have all the psychological and educative value of a hobby, especially when success was crowned by badges awarded after passing tests and examinations. Many people took up their lifelong professions in the first place because of hobbies, because of what psychologists call centers of interest. I have met serious geographers who began life with no more than a stamp collection and geologists who found their vocation by collecting stones. One of the best specialists in American Indian culture, Paul Coze, simply followed the path pointed out to him as a boy by a very "redskin" form of scouting.

I have always been very sorry for those very serious men who have no hobbies. They can look forward to an old age when they will be bored and annoying to others. I can think of an example at once! A friend who is a little older than I, a very good husband, a good father, a hard worker, and an excellent citizen. A man who is a bit too perfect. There were three centers of interest in his life—family, work, and local politics. He gave himself wholly to all three. Now he is old and he suffers from poor health. His children have gone their various ways. He has retired from his work. Because of his health he can no longer take part in local politics. He literally does not know what to do with himself. He is bored all day long and as a result his health is getting worse. Those near to him are suffering because he is suffering. If only he had a hobby—even if it was only collecting match-boxes!

I often think of him together with my father and compare them both in old age. My father was also too serious and weighed down by his work. But he had at least one passionate hobby—gardening—and that kept him well and sane. He belonged to the generation that had just come from the country to the towns in search of work, and so he retained a taste for the earth. It was for this generation that far-seeing philanthropists provided allotments. My father had an almost physical need to fork and dig, water and prune. As soon as he was free for a moment or two, he was out into the garden. At first he had a little allotment of a few square yards, but as soon as he could afford it he had a house with quite a large piece of land, which soon became a pleasure garden, a vegetable garden, and an orchard.

Although he was not a man of robust health, he was vigorous enough in old age and I attribute this to his passion for gardening. I am also sure that it was gardening that made him so balanced both physically and morally. A couple of hours in his garden made up for numerous troubles. And God knows, he had enough of those! I was more inclined to intellectual pursuits and did not inherit my father's hobby. I have come to regret it. And while on the subject of gardening, it is important to recognize that it is not exclusively masculine. Many women have a natural taste for it or else acquire it. In England there are countless keen women gardeners—so many in fact that Englishmen are reduced to mowing the lawn.

Many Frenchmen, on the other hand, love doing odd jobs at home. They seem to have to work with pieces of metal or wood, knock in nails, turn screwdrivers, hang wallpaper, and do wiring. It benefits both them and their homes. Husbands whose work is intellectual relax by using their hands and the physical energy that is not consumed during the day.

One of the most curious hobbies that I have ever come across is the building of model railways—not only locomotives, trucks, and carriages, but also complete railway lines with points, automatic changing, stations, and even derailments and accidents. This hobby almost always goes back to childhood. I have met adults who meet regularly once a week to play at railways together. One group of model railway enthusiasts I knew included important, high-ranking men in industry and society, leading doctors and members of the establishment on the one hand and ordinary working men—most of them railway or ex-railway employees—on the other. The latter were so keen on their work that they could not forget it even in their leisure time. Others, of course, are dedicated to gliding or sailing. These are not, however, occupations that are suitable for people of advanced years.

While we are on the subject of hobbies, we should not, of course, forget collectors and their collections. How many different things there are to collect! I have come across collectors of jewels, weapons, old books, ceramics and china, snuff-boxes, match-boxes, posters, cheese-boxes, lead soldiers, tin soldiers and wooden soldiers and, it is hardly necessary to add, stamps, paintings, and old prints. Some people even collect chamber pots.

No one ever became a collector just by wanting to be one. You have to have a vocation, and that is usually present from childhood onwards and begins with collecting marbles or stamps. Collecting is a hobby like any other, but it requires time, room, and quite often money as well. It depends on what you collect, but a collection can bring a great deal of intellectual satisfaction and may even contribute to human culture. Since 1923, I have been accumulating picture postcards of all the places that I have visited. I hardly ever look at them now, but the time may come when my legs will no longer be able to take me where I want to go and I shall only be able to travel by looking at my collection.

I could go on forever listing hobbies, but I will end by mentioning one which I have never had myself, but which seems to me to have a great deal of human interest—amateur radio. It has all the pleasure of doing odd jobs, but, when it comes to broadcasting and receiving on the set you have made yourself, there is also the very special pleasure of human contact with other radio amateurs all over the world. Friendships far beyond the seas and mountains have been formed in this way with people you will never see, although you can meet them every day on the air and sometimes even perform important services for them. Almost all the radio amateurs I have known have been outstanding because of their qualities of mind and heart. (I am not speaking, of course, of spies—they are professionals, not amateurs.)

It is, in the end, not very important which hobby you choose. What is important is to have one—or several.

Serving Others

"I told you that you were an Epicurean! All that you can do is suggest selfish pleasures, compensations, and hobbies! "Smoking his pipe and looking at his roses! What a limited ideal! And how lower middle class!"

"I could hardly suggest to old men and women that they should go out and lead a revolution, could I? That is something that they would not want or be able to do at their age. You need great energy, a few illusions, and the whole of the future before you to be a revolutionary. An old man may have revolutionary ideas, but young people will have to carry out the revolution that he is thinking about."

"Maybe. But I still think that what you are suggesting is very lower middle class."

"No it isn't—it's just human. All you have to be to take pleasure in looking at your roses is a human being with eyes and a sense of smell. The middle class—upper, professional, or lower—has nothing to do with the flower. All that I am advising old people to do is to gather the simple, modest pleasures that God offers them."

"Gather! Gather the roses of life while you can. And you call yourself a Christian! You ought to reread the Gospels."

"I have read and reread them. I have found the cross in them, but I have also found the beatitudes, the lilies of the fields, and the birds of the air. I admit that my advice may give scandal to puritans and Jansenists. But what of it! There were, after all, people like Monsieur Hamon among the gentlemen of Port-Royal, who loved flowers and gathered simple pleasures. Don't forget too that the Good News is a message of happiness."

"I agree. But it is not a tranquil, narrow, selfish, and exclusive joy."

"I agree with you! But let me finish. The Gospels tell us to love God our Father and to show him that we love him by loving our brothers. Loving is doing good to the one you love. If I may say so, we can only do good to God by loving our brothers and serving them. And disinterested service is one of the noblest of human joys. And, what is more, I am quite convinced that you can go on serving others even in old age. Now listen to my sermon."

* * *

To serve others you must be available and your service must be gratuitous.

To be available to others means that you must have free time and that you must have a free spirit. Professional work and family responsibilities are undoubtedly necessary and preeminent forms of service. But the time that they take and the anxieties and the worries to which they give rise certainly restrict the possibility of other forms of service. When you are old, you are released from the daily round of tasks and you no longer have a job to do. You have handed your family responsibilities on to your grown up children. So, as far as time and your imagination are concerned, you are once again your own master. That means that, if you are still generous in spirit, you can use this new freedom to serve your fellowmen and do something for them that you always wanted to do when you were younger, but could never do because of pressure of time and other responsibilities.

You can still be politically and socially militant—not, of course, as a young or middle-aged person would be, but in a way that is suitable to your age and condition. And your service must be gratuitous. You must give it without reward. You place yourself at your brother's disposition simply because he is your brother. You have no ulterior motive and you expect nothing in return. It is not possible to give this kind of gratuitous service when you are working professionally. You work then to earn a crust of bread and perhaps a bit of butter and jam on it. When you are retired and have no profession, however, you can give for nothing, even if your means only allow you to give very little, and you can serve others for nothing. What an unexpected pleasure that is! I have often wondered if, in our consumer society, in which you don't get or do anything for nothing, one of the most important social and spiritual tasks that old people can do is to bear gratuitous witness to gratuitous service. The old man or woman can become the one who serves from love alone, just as Christ served us by giving his life for us.

* * *

I can already hear several old people complaing: I would love to serve others and I suffer continuously because I feel so useless. But whom can I serve? And in what way? I have often offered, but no one wants my services. I have been thrown on the rubbish heap.

There is a great deal of truth in this objection. Many younger people regard the aged *a priori* as worn out and useless and think that it might be wrong to throw them in the dustbin, but that their real place is the junk cupboard, together with chipped china or the junk room with its old boxes and trunks full of all kinds of odds and ends. At the same time, I think my dear old friends who complain in this way ought to examine their consciences.

Have you, in offering your services, not wanted perhaps to dominate others? Perhaps you were hardly conscious of this—maybe quite unconscious. Did you not want to impose yourself on others or at least impose some of your views on them? I am thinking especially of the relationships between elderly parents and their offspring with young families. And old, experienced workers with long service in an organization that has changed—not only its staff, but also its methods and even its aims. The old person ought to serve humbly—and humility is a gratuitous form of service. I know how hard that can be, but I think it is best to resign oneself to it. Perhaps you should not just wait for invitations and congratulations to come to you. You might try asking people to let you serve them in ways that they want. And don't take offence! However strange it may seem and however much men may need each other, it is never easy to serve others. You have to be recognized and accepted as a servant. Jesus understood this—he came, not to be served, but to serve.

Despite all these difficulties, I still believe that the old person has a part to play in society. He is no longer now what he was in the past, in a traditional agricultural society, nor is he the same as he was in the previous century, which was a time of transition. But he does seem to be as necessary as he always was. Or as she always was. Let us examine this more closely.

* * *

In the scattered and fragmented family life of today, the elders—grandparents and some aunts and uncles—so long as they have retained the secret of communion with young people represent the past, continuity and, to use a word that has often been wrongly applied, tradition. Children know this instinctively and seem to go on questioning their grandparents until they are at least twelve. How many times I must have asked my grandfather to tell me about his war—the Franco-Prussian

War of 1870. His ear was frost-bitten at the front. I don't know why I was so impressed by his frost-bitten ear, but I do know that I never stopped asking him about it. When I was a teen-ager, I turned away from the past and was fascinated by the future, but the memory of my grandfather, the war of 1870, and the frost-bitten ear were ineradicable.

Then we have grandmother doing what the French, with their passion for English words, call baby-sitting and replacing the parents for a few hours. If the children are old enough, she sheds memories of her own younger days all around her. And grandfather taking his grandchildren for a time to his home in the country and initiating them into the secrets of nature and the mysteries of fishing. They have a part to play in family life! They may not even be conscious of it, but it is no less important for that. They can give these young and impressionable minds memories that will last forever.

In the Soviet Union, I am told, the best allies and the worst enemies of the regime are the grannies or babushkas. They help the regime because they make the children aware of the real progress made since the Revolution, but they are its enemies because they teach them to say their prayers and, when they are baby-sitting, they sit in front of icons.

Even in our urban civilization, some families still continue to go to the grandparents on important occasions such as Christmas. There is nothing like it for uniting the tribe and giving everyone a sense of belonging to each other. This kind of family get-together reminds me of an old lady I knew with so many children, grandchildren, and great grandchildren that it was difficult for her to find her direction among them. When her husband died, she went to live in a large country house which was always open to everyone. One day, when almost the whole of her great family was there, she made this charming statement: "I do love it when you come here. It amuses me. But

I don't like too many of you all at once. No more than thirty at a time." She would have been surprised if anyone had called her a matriarch, but she was one, of course, in the deepest sense of the word. She would even have been astonished if she had been told that she fulfilled an important social function. But she did. She simply lived and loved.

Women enjoy writing more than men, and they do it more easily and more simply. Letter-writing has always been a female form of literature—Madame de Sévigné bears witness to that. Grandmothers often write better letters and more of them than girls and grown up women because they have more time. Even in a telephone age like our own—and grandmothers also make use of the instrument!—letters containing trifling yet precious details help to preserve family ties. Go on writing letters, grandmothers, go on spreading news among the family! Be a hyphen between all the members of your own family and you will in your old age complete your life's work by keeping the flame of love alive.

I have used the word "hyphen" and it seems to me to describe very well the part played in the family by the old members. They are disinterested and wise, and this makes it possible for them to act as peacemakers in family quarrels—those little conflicts that can cause such great suffering in all families if they are left to grow, harden, and take root. Despite all the great social changes that have taken place, family situations, the conflicts between the sexes and different generations and the jealousies and the conflicting interests seem to have remained, perhaps not identical, but at least very similar. The older members have all experienced these conflicts and have managed, somehow or other, to get through. Because their experience is human, it remains valuable. A piece of good advice or a soothing word can often turn aside a misunderstanding or a conflict that may be as painful as it is unnecessary.

On the other hand, if a grandparent tries to exert an excessive influence, a situation that might have been settled of its own accord may be made much worse. I am thinking here of those assiduous mothers-in-law who, even in old age, cannot accept their sons or daughters-in-law. I have known those who have moved heaven and earth to get their sons married to certain girls or have done the opposite and gone as far as they could to separate an engaged couple or even work energetically for a divorce. Old women should be aware of the terrifying power wielded by their tongues. They should not use that power to divide and spread hatred, but to unite and increase love.

* * *

The influence of a good family makes itself felt in the whole neighborhood. This is as true of an old couple as it is of a young family. It may be even more true, since old people have more free time and are less inclined to remain enclosed within the family group. The tendency to segregate people of different ages, which is so much a feature of modern city life, is therefore all the more to be regretted. Real life is a constant encounter between different sexes, ages, professions, and social groups. Young families and old people need each other, if only in order to serve each other in little ways.

The part played by women in the neighborhood is, of course, very important—as important as her part in the family. She maintains all the essential links. What an essential place those old concierges had in the blocks of flats in Paris and Lyon. Some of them, it is true, were too curious, tactless, and talkative. As we used to say in Lyon, they would have made the Blessed Virgin fight Saint Joseph. Their quarters provided a permanent and certain shelter for discord. But others created a different climate in their houses—one of togetherness and understanding. They knew everyone in the building and even in the neighborhood. They were able to give you the information you wanted straightaway. Although they knew everything, they watched their tongues and said nothing—or not very much. They kept an eye on the kids playing in the courtyard or the street and, when they went too far, they would tell their parents. They did all this simply and naturally without even knowing that they were bearing witness to charity.

I am very grateful to many of these good women. In fact, I would go completely counter to the common opinion and gladly pay homage to the concierge. She belongs to the past now and has disappeared from the scene, but there are still elderly women in those blocks of flats which still provide them, for better or for worse, with shelter. Even in the middle-class premises in Paris, with residents who hardly know each other and who do no more than simply greet each other, anonymously, on the stairs, there are old ladies who are concerned about the fate of their fellow-tenants and perform little services for them.

* * *

But the old person's role in society goes beyond these narrow confines. The most able-bodied and the most capable can always occupy themselves serving their contemporaries who are less able-bodied. They have to organize themselves in order to break through their solitude, alleviate their misery and discomfort, and obtain justice and recognition. This means that they should form associations expressing their solidarity and their just claims. Who else will make those claims for them? Only they can do it and then only while they still have the strength—both physically and in numbers. They will not, of course, achieve their aims alone. They will have to be helped by younger people. But nothing would be more harmful and humiliating for them than passivity. Ought they really, at their age, become no more than the subjects or the objects—

whichever you like—of paternalistic or maternalistic treatment? Even in the homes for the elderly there are opportunities for them to organize themselves, if only to plan their leisure time activities. The younger people who serve the aged in various ways—all good ways—should have one thing constantly in mind—to interest the old people for whom they are caring in working together responsibly for others. Those in charge of old people are really devoted, but behind that devotion there is all to often an authoritarian attitude and the old person is treated like a child and humiliated.

Old people have to form pressure groups, then, in order to influence public opinion and the powers that be. If the politicians are not to make use of them for their own ends, those groups have to be administered and directed by the old people themselves. These associations are necessary for the old people to help each other in a spirit of solidarity and for this reason it is highly desirable for the members to play an active part in them and not simply receive what the organizations can give them. It may, of course, be difficult for the whole structure to be administered by old people, but it should not be impossible for some of the old members—those with the physical strength and ability—to be employed at least part time. This in itself would be a form of service.

* * *

To stop at that point would be a sign of collective selfishness. Old people have a certain freedom, because they are able to determine their own hours of work. Because of this, I think they can fulfill one task which in the past was regarded as purely charitable, but which nowadays has a really social dimension. That task is visiting.

What does the word mean? What is visiting? It means simply visiting those who need to be visited because they are lonely. Not only those old people who are shut up in homes or in their own flats or rooms, but also those who are unable to get out at all. That means those of every age in ordinary hospitals or psychiatric wards as well as prisoners. It means, in other words, everyone who has been abandoned by the world or left to the care of official organizations. We old people can visit all those who may be bitter because they have so few human contacts and who want to be recognized and treated as human beings, even though they may appear not to.

There have always been many elderly members of the Saint Vincent de Paul Society who have done a great deal of visiting. The methods and the work of the Society and similar organizations have changed radically because of the changes that have taken place in misery itself. Many forms of suffering have disappeared and others, often more subtle, have replaced them. We no longer live at the time when Sister Rosalie Rendu made use of people's good will to relieve the misery of the working classes and the unemployed in the Mouffetard district, at the time of coupons for bread and coal. But there is still a great deal of misery everywhere—and not just in the countries of the so-called Third World. In almost every big town there are countless people who are isolated who want us to respect and love them. Many of them desperately need our help and guidance through the legal and administrative labyrinth of modern society, just in order to obtain the rights to which they are entitled, but which they are not capable of claiming themselves. They are waiting for us to visit them. And in this context, the old word "visit" is the right one. Should we keep them waiting? Or should we just leave the monopoly of generosity to young people, who lack the time and the experience that we have?

It is not just the man who hasn't enough money to keep himself alive who is poor. It is also the one who needs his brothers in order to live materially, intellectually, or spiritually. We are, from this point of view, all more or less poor or more or less rich and if we have a surplus of one or other material or spiritual commodity, we should not think that it belongs exclusively to us. We should share it with our brothers, in a division that will make all men equal at a really deep level.

You still have a great deal to give, old people! Give and go on giving in the little time that you still have left to you. You will then have the satisfaction of serving others.

I make this appeal to all old people, but even more especially perhaps to those who have experience in administration and finance. Retired civil servants, accountants and others can give incalculable service to all kinds of associations of a political, social, or religious nature. As secretaries and treasurers, they can do what young or middle-aged men cannot always do, the first because they lack the experience and the second because they lack the time. They can continue or even begin to be active and perhaps militant politically and socially in the humble and possibly thankless position of honorary secretary or treasurer. It may not be a glorious or powerful function, but it is very useful and indeed essential. Another very simple but important service that can be carried out by retired people is at the information or reception desk for visitors to various organizations or, of course, the telephone enquiry service. Voluntary, unpaid service is, I know, looked down on nowadays, but it is not synonymous with incompetence and many organizations and associations are bound to rely on those who work for nothing and often with great skill and devotion, if they are to preserve their independence.

I could give countless examples of such services rendered by retired public servants, lawyers, social workers, and nurses. I have known old retired teachers, lay people, and sisters, who have preserved their love of teaching to the very end and have therefore voluntarily taught groups of young people in their neighborhood, succeeding as well as they did when they were younger. How many young men have not learned Latin, for example, especially in the rural parts of France, from a retired parish priest who taught it when he was younger?

I will confine myself to only three examples—all people I have known personally. The first is an elderly lady who had an intuitive and indeed almost instinctive grasp of what others needed in the way of care. She learned how to give injections. (They have completely replaced cupping and the enemas of long ago and are used just as much, perhaps more!) She became the traveling medical service in a large village where there was no nurse of any kind. Both the local doctor and the sick trusted her. She bathed, bandaged, and injected to the end of her life. She was a very ordinary woman in every way and she would have been surprised if she had been told that she was fulfilling a social function.

My second example is a retired engineer who had held various leading posts in heavy industry. He was an active Christian who had always hoped to perform other, more direct services to others. As soon as he retired, he came to me and offered me ten years of his life, taking over the administration of the journal *Chronique Sociale* and all its ramifications. I had found it a tedious and too time-consuming task, and I accepted his offer at once. He kept his word. At the end of his promised ten years, we both stood down and gave way to younger people. He is now working for *La Vie Montante,* and I have become a priest.

My last example is a friend whose son is a priest in the southern part of the Rhône Valley. He is widowed and lives with his son. He is very active, providing a permanent, almost round the clock service. The priests who are members of the team are always on the move and he is what mathematicians would call the fixed point or, to use another metaphor, the pivot. He always knows where each priest is at any moment and he stays in the house to receive visitors and calls and to provide information. In other words, he goes on serving after a life of service.

But we old men and women can also serve on local councils. I am not thinking here of those old political die-hards who might do better to think of their own last days and their relationship with God than to continue, by force of habit, in political activity when really they no longer understand very much of it. I am in fact thinking of much humbler forms of service. It is often difficult to recruit sufficient people for service on the smaller councils in villages and towns. People with full-time jobs may have the best will in the world, but they lack the time to devote to council and committee meetings and so, as long as they are still vigorous and wide awake, old people can be a real godsend in the local community. In fact, if they are unwilling to offer their services, they can be accused of laziness and selfishness.

* * *

It has to be said again and again in a very loud voice, emphatically and insistently: Old age does not mean that one ceases to serve others. One may, I agree, have to serve in different ways, but one still needs to serve and one still has a duty to serve. Those who have served actively and vigorously should not be discouraged when they feel old age approaching. There is still plenty for them to do—for their brothers. And as for those who have never served their brothers very much when they were young or middle-aged—it is never too late to begin. There are always late vocations, both in the religious and in the lay sense, and there are always workers taken on at the eleventh hour.

You Have To Prepare for Old Age

I have given you an idea of most of the occupations and activities open to you in old age. The obvious conclusion to be drawn is that you cannot leave it to chance. If you want to spend your last years well, you have to prepare for them a long time in advance. If you don't plan your old age, it will just come upon you one day without warning and you won't know what to do about it.

Don't exaggerate what I am saying. I don't think, for example, that you should begin to consider your old age when you are twenty or even when you are thirty. As the book of Ecclesiastes tells us, there is a time for everything. To put this thought in another way, we can say that there is, in every person's life, a time for looking at the future and another when you should live from day to day without worrying about tomorrow and the day after. You may be conscious of the first signs of growing old. I would advise you then to regard them as an alarm signal and to begin your preparations for old age, which may come all too quickly. They are the first signs of winter and frost, and it is time to lay in provisions.

I am not suggesting that you should imitate those public servants of earlier generations who thought of nothing but retirement, as a kind of paradise. They began to feel really happy at fifty-five, sixty, or sixty-five, depending on their work or their status. While they were waiting for retirement, they went into hibernation, like dormice. Then, quite often, when they thought that they were within reach of happiness, they found they had nothing at all in their hands. A song that was popular before the First World War made gentle fun of this attitude:

> It may be a bit boring,
> but it's certainly not dull—
> when you've reached the age of sixty,
> you retire!

Nor should you imitate those old skinflints who go on stuffing sovereigns and crowns into a woolen stocking or a piggy-bank to provide for their last years. These people have been miserly since their earliest years, and they stay like that to the end. They have never lived. I am not suggesting that Molière's avaricious Harpagon or Père Gaspard should be your model. If I wanted to find real examples, I would look for the lilies of the field, as the Gospel suggests. And a little further on: "Let the day's trouble be sufficient for the day."

But however disinterested we may be or completely abandoned to God's providence, we must have some foresight. I know, of course, that Isabelle Rivière used to sing about our duty not to have foresight, if only not to be a burden on others. Foresight is a requirement of justice and charity. Preparing for old age is not simply a question of taking out life insurances and contributing to a pension fund. It also means knowing what you will do when you have to admit that you are old. You have to train for old age, as a new situation that you cannot avoid or reject.

We have first of all to determine approximately the age for

retirement, although this may, of course, be fixed by our employers. I would stress that this can only be approximate. We are, after all, not always in control of our situation in life and cannot make absolute decisions. But we ought to have in mind an ultimate date, beyond which we hope we shall not go.

Then we should look out for the place where we shall land. Where do we want to go? What sort of occupations do we want? Shall we still be able to serve others and how shall we do it? In some cases, it is better to break completely with the past, move from the place where we have spent our adult, working years and give up all the activities that we have had. In other cases, such a total break would be dangerous and we might do better to stay in the same place and not let go of all the things that we have done in the past. It is important to think carefully about your own situation now and in the future before making any decisions.

You do not, I should add, take these decisions in isolation. If you are married, they have to be taken together with your wife. If you have a family, they also concern your children. To some extent, they also concern your friends. Your decisions, therefore, have to be—to use the word that became fashionable during the Second Vatican Council—collegial. They take time. So you must make them at the right time.

Above all, face up to old age. Think calmly and courageously about it. Don't regret the past. And don't be bitter. Very soon, old age will not be in the future—it will be your present. It will be your present with God and you will have to live and, if possible, be happy. Your happiness will have to be in accordance with the human condition. It will always, of course, be a relative happiness and exposed to chance,but it will still be the happiness that God wants you to have—he, after all, only wants his creatures to be happy. The future slips away ahead of us and the past no longer belongs to us. So we are right to live all the more intensely in the present. You are on the threshold of old age, but you still have the present, while preparing for the future.

I am not suggesting that your old age should be programmed. However much I may believe that programming, as it is called, is necessary in our modern economy, I know from experience that to impose too precise a program on personal life often results in a fiasco. You can and ought to make plans, so long as they are not based on pipedreams and illusions. Working out a program for your old age is not necessarily the same as drawing plans for castles in Spain, especially if you remember that you may have to change the plans. You cannot always have the old age that you have planned. You will, however, generally have the one for which you have prepared. And plans form part of that preparation.

Pessimists will point out the uncertainties and the risks involved. Is it not futile, they will say, to prepare yourself for a future that you do not possess? What use are even the most reasonable plans if you have a coronary thrombosis tomorrow or a car accident? Both would put an end to all your plans and you as well. I agree entirely with you, of course, if you say that. Any one of us can be struck down by illness or an accident and all of us can be the victims together of an economic crisis or a nuclear war.

> No—the future belongs to no one!
> The future belongs to God!

Of course it does. The words of the song are true, but what about it? Just because we have no certainty about our own future, does that mean we should not prepare for it? "The best laid schemes o' mice an' men," the Scottish poet said, "Gang aft agley," but is the possibility of failure a good reason for not planning at all? The river of time may not flow in exactly the same direction as our will, but do we always have to go along with the stream? Does not man's real greatness consist in his never ceasing to look, despite all his failures and disappointments, for mastery of what he cannot naturally control? If we are deterred by the chance that we shall be frustrated, we shall in the end be led to give up everything and above all God. We should not be anxious about tomorrow—we should prepare for it. We should do everything that is within our power and leave it to God to do—or not to do—the rest, according to his will.

We cannot avoid old age and especially our own. But to a very great extent we make our own old age and, as a result, make it our own, so long as we prepare for it. This is my advice to all of you in your fifties and sixties.

The Positive Values of Old Age

One of the best ways of preparing for old age is to think about its positive values and, by meditation, learn to appreciate them more. It is, after all, too often forgotten in the modern world that old age has many genuinely human values.

Values are both spiritual qualities and norms by which we can make judgements, and they can be found at every age of life. The values of childhood are simplicity, innocence, an ignorance of evil, a fresh way of seeking the world, and a purity of emotional response. Jesus invited us to learn again this spirit of childhood when he made children stand in the midst of his apostles and presented them to them as a model.

The values of youth are vitality, a militant spirit, generosity, enthusiasm, and indignation. These are all qualities that we regret so much when we think about our adolescence and remember when we were in our twenties.

When we were in our maturity, we were above all rational, persevering, realistic, and responsible. We accepted life and the tasks it imposed on us.

The child is not yet aware of the weight of human responsibilities, and that makes him light, free, lively, and at everyone's disposition. The young man thinks that he is weighed down with responsibilities, but he is mistaken and rushes forward to pick up heavy burdens. The mature man bears them without flinching and goes straight ahead with a measured pace.

I can hear you objecting—there is no particular merit in any of these qualities that man has at different ages, because they are simply what they are and no more. My reply to this objection is that this idea of merit is not very precise because it is confused with the overcoming of difficulties and because, in the end, it is not very important for us to define it. Psychologists and moralists have the task of defining values and we must leave it to God to assess their merits.

I am speaking just now of taking up burdens. An old man cannot carry what he was so eager to bear as a young man and what he bore so doggedly when he was older. There comes a time in everyone's life when he no longer has the strength to bear burdens alone. He can, however, help others to test their weight and carry them, like Simon of Cyrene helping Christ to carry the cross. This is one of the deepest values of old age. In folk wisdom, the old man has always been seen as wise and benevolent. I do not think that folk wisdom is wrong here, and the values of wisdom and benevolence have the guarantee of authenticity. The old man is normally wise—despite the existence of old fools of the kind that we have all known. Old age has no miraculous property that enables it automatically to straighten twisted spirits and fill idiots with intelligence. And I would not deny that it emphasizes not only the physical features of a man's face, making him sometimes a caricature of his younger self, but also aspects of his inner nature. An old fool seems more foolish than a silly young man because he no longer has the excuse of youth. An old idiot seems more absurd than a young blockhead because he talks more, and more stupidly.

But I don't want to talk about the exceptions, however many there may be. I am thinking here of the development of normal people. It would seem that most old men no longer want to be carried away by the enthusiasms of youth and that they cling less stubbornly to their mistakes than middle-aged men. They have, in other words, become wise. They have learned the art of living. Their judgement is more balanced. They behave more correctly. They reflect, compare, and wait before making a decision. They appreciate the taste of material and spiritual foods. In the past, old people expressed themselves proverbially—a clear sign of their folk wisdom.

Old age has had to pay a great price for this wisdom—the price of human experience that is always painful and, at least in certain respects, disappointing. Old people know how to bear burdens because their shoulders and backs have been bruised by them. They have been tested in ways that prove how much a person is worth—love, work, illness, failure, solitude, and the death of those they love. These ordeals have forced them to reveal themselves and show what was in them—whether they had, in the popular phrase, any guts or not. Old men have had to go through the ordeal of fire and be burnt, and they bear on the bodies and in their souls the traces of those burns. How many old men alive today have been through those great collective ordeals—the war, for example, at the front or as prisoners-of-war? I can never thank the Lord enough for having let me go through the astonishing experience of the First World War and imprisonment and then the Resistance Movement in the Second World War, without staining my hands with blood. It made a man of me.

One of the consequences of this kind of experience is that we are left feeling weary and bitter, and if these feelings last, we may be broken forever. If we overcome them, we may become wise, even though our body may bear painful scars. We shall, in our wisdom, know what life is and what men are like. We shall have lost our childish innocence but have gained the innocence of wisdom. We shall no longer have the illusions of youth, who believe that the world began when they were born, and we shall not experience the proud self-satisfaction of middle age. But we shall respect life and our fellow man and women.

We have a duty to communicate our wisdom to others and share it with them. We have to give it generously so that they may benefit from it. Do not misunderstand me! I don't think at all that we should crush them beneath the weight of our experience—they would tell us to go to blazes and take our experience with us! Nor do I think we should try to strip them of all their cherished ideas and make them artificially and prematurely old—that would be treating them badly.

Some kinds of advice are detestable. For example: "You'll find out when you are my age!" Poor fellow! He'll find out soon enough! And then the habit of beginning every sentence with an annoying phrase such as: "When I was your age," or "In the old days." And how intensely irritating it is for the listener if we keep repeating old memories! The old soldier who goes on forever and ever about his campaigns is only showing us that he has finished forever with campaigning. I think it is wise to keep those stories for regimental reunions.

Communicating wisdom is altogether more subtle. It is done almost unconsciously by providing a living example, by disinterested conversations, and by giving advice, above all, at the right moment, when the other person is ready to receive it. And above all, of course, when he asks you for it. Or when you are both talking in a jocular fashion and pretending not to be too serious.

The gifts of wisdom and counsel both come, of course, from the Holy Spirit. So let us allow the Spirit to act through us as he wants to.

* * *

Wisdom and benevolence go hand in hand. Young men and women are hard and intolerant. It is good that they are. If they were not there would be no flow of wholesome, salty water to prevent the human race from stagnating. They are always in revolt, and they refuse to compromise and in this way remind us of the demands made by absolute values. Middle age is, in its own way, as hard as youth. At that age, men have discovered the pleasure of settled existence and the need for compromise, but they are often far too oriented toward usefulness. They want everything to be immediately effective and reject anything that does not seem to fit in with their aims. They also always give very convincing reasons for their rejections!

The old man is usually more benevolent. He puts up with much more. This may, of course, be because his suprarenal glands do not produce enough adrenalin to arouse anger, but it is, I think, mainly because he is made more tender and understanding by wisdom. He knows man, and he no longer expects so much from him as the young man expects. He knows how relative all human endeavors are and how much they depend on chance, and he is no longer prepared to sacrifice human beings on the altar of achievement when he knows from his own experience that they can suffer.

You must put up with my confessions! I was terribly intolerant as a young man. I may have understood the desire for usefulness and compromise a bit better than other young men, because I was brought up in the southern part of the Rhône Valley, a part of France where those qualities are known from birth. But I just could not endure the slightest gap between expressing the thought and carrying out the action. It seemed to me to be inconsistent at least and even the height of hypocrisy not to act at once. To delay filled me with nausea. I quite respected people who sinned half-heartedly, but did not for a moment suspect that I could also be half-hearted.

As soon as I discovered them, I read the works of Léon Bloy

avidly. In his raging passion, he seemed to be expressing all my own anger and loathing. Have I been changed by old age? Probably not, at least in the depths of my being. I am still repelled by inconsistency and hypocrisy. But I am no longer angry. Instead of anger, I feel an immense pity. This may be because I have had to take account of my own lack of logic and above all of what separates my thoughts from my actions. But it is also, I think, because I have over the years come to understand man's weakness, his blindness to himself, his wretchedness and his nothingness. Bernanos wrote about the "gentle pity of God." I have for a long time wanted men to have pity on me, so how could I not have pity on them? Very many questionable things are taking place now in the world and in the Church and I must be honest—very few of them can still surprise me. I go on reading Léon Bloy, but I feel more at home with the old author—an old lion still roaring, but not so fierce—than with the young man spewing out wrongs and injustices like a gargoyle pouring rain-water from a cathedral roof onto the heads of the passersby.

Let me go on with my confession. I was dedicated to argument and, although I was often funny and seldom malicious, I could be hard, violent, and acrimonious. I liked to reduce my opponents to silence, put them in a position where it was impossible for them to reply, make them contradict themselves and get caught up in absurd statements. This was not, I think, because I was naturally wicked, but because I was excessively aggressive, loved fighting and, I have to admit it, took a delight in winning. I had ample opportunity to develop my aggression in the public debates that were so popular when I was young, and it may be that I was all the more violently aggressive because I seemed so restrained. I used to keep calm. I was very polite with my opponents, but I did not spare them when they made mistakes or said silly things. I liked knocking them out with apparently gentle blows.

Nowadays, I sometimes still have to take part in arguments, but I no longer believe in the virtues of polemics and in any case I have lost the taste for them. I always seem to understand anyone who wants to argue with me too well even to want to crush him or even to catch him out. I prefer to reply with silence, as Christ replied to his judges after he had said what he had to say. Now, if my opponent makes a serious or even a crude mistake, I don't get angry. He arouses my sense of pity. After all, I have often made mistakes, too, and I am still making them.

I have confided in you, and surely you can do the same, on the basis of your own experience. Bad-tempered old men and sharp old women—I don't need anyone to tell me about these! I have seen enough blotched old faces with enough purple in them to indicate an imminent stroke and thin, tight lips concealing a spiteful tongue. But I like to think that these are exceptions. Age teaches us benevolence and makes us tolerant, because as we grow older we realize that we dare not demand from others what we ourselves cannot give. We prefer silence to outbrusts of fury, even if our silence is disapproving. We treat the people who annoy us with sweetness rather than with sharp words when we are old.

You old people I have loved—I cannot forget your faces or your words! Your restful appearance, your slow, wise way of speaking, your constantly forgiving attitude. I have often made you suffer because I was so violent. You never told me, and I was hardly conscious of it—sometimes I caught a glimpse of sadness in your eyes. I would like to be like you, wise and benevolent, in my old age. And I would like all my old friends to be like you.

O Spirit of Love

O Holy Spirit, Spirit of love,
tireless giver living in our souls in order to make us conform to the Man-God
and to bring us as adopted sons to the Father's glorious love,
I stretch out my old, clumsy hands to you.
Pour into them the treasure of your gifts.

In my youth, you gave me the gift of strength.
"I am writing to you, young men, because you are strong," the old man, Saint John, said.
With your strength, I have fought against giants and demons,
I have crossed rivers and seas and have climbed mountains.
I have experienced victory and defeat in turn.
But with your strength I have also stood up after every fall.
And I have gone on fighting.

In my mature years, you gave me the gift of knowledge.
Through you, I plunged down into the abyss and entered the infinite space of heaven.
Through you, I learned the secrets of nature and the human heart.
Through you, I perceived the depths of the deity.
Through you, I was thrilled with the joy of knowledge.

O Holy Spirit, in my old age, give me the gift of wisdom and benevolence, wisdom's companion.
Through you, let me taste the fruit of the tree of life and enable others to taste it.
Through you, let me no longer be surprised by anything, but let me go on admiring.

Let me not try to be understood, but to understand.
Let my words be distilled and made into the pure golden liquid of living truth.
Let me always forgive others infinitely and not demand forgiveness from them—let me be satisfied with your forgiveness.
Let me give counsel and respect my brothers' freedom.
Let me live fully in the present and only look forward to eternity.

O Holy Spirit, may your dew and your fire rain on my old heart,
so that it is full of that love
which is the only true wisdom.

Amen

The Old Man and the Child

There is a close relationship between the old man and the child. This is something that all grandfathers and grandmothers know and that makes many fathers and mothers experience a twinge of jealousy.

The child loves the old man because he instinctively knows that the old man is forgiving and tolerant and because he senses in him a weakness that is similar to his own. And the old man loves the child because childhood radiates light and warmth and because the child has come from his own flesh and carries within him the only future in time that remains to him. I am sorry for the old man who has no children around him—he is without the last happiness that life can offer. And the child who has never known the tenderness of an old man will always have a gap in his life—an emptiness that may prevent his emotions and affections from reaching maturity.

The child is never irritated by the old man's faults. He is not wearied by his grandfather or grandmother telling the same story for the hundredth time. He likes being told the same story in exactly the same way and with exactly the same words. This is clear from Charles Perrault's transcriptions of Mother Goose's Tales.

Nor is the old man ever discouraged by the child's faults. He is glad to let his weakness rest against the weakness of someone else who needs him. He relives the memories of his own childhood through the medium of the child.

The old man and the child often quarrel, of course, and the grown up daughter who is now a mother whispers: "I really don't know which one of the two is the child." But these quarrels do not last, because both the old man and the child have the same power to forget very quickly. How many times I squabbled with my grandmother, for instance! But our quarrels did not prevent us from loving each other.

I very much resent the way modern society has separated people of different ages. With cruel insensitivity, it has deprived both the old man and the child of a great human joy. In an old people's home, grandfather or grandmother is simply a stranger whom the child visits occasionally, when the parents think of it, and the visit is usually a bleak experience. Then, one day, the child may go with a group of cars to the cemetery, thinking of something else on the way.

You old men—and women, of course—who have been able to remain in touch with your grandchildren—or just with children, your friend's or your neighbor's—you should thank God for your good fortune and make the most of those precious moments when the two extremities of life are in contact with each other, to the mutual benefit of both. Grandfathers and grandmothers—tell the little ones who are listening to you at those times the stories of your youth or just any stories you like. The time will come, all too quickly, when they will think that they are men and women and then they will not listen to you any more.

If we are to believe Victor Hugo, there is an art in being a grandparent. I don't know whether he practiced that art as well as he wrote about it, but he did write about it and we should be grateful to him for it. The art of being a grandfather is first and foremost being patient and forgiving. It is also paying attention to the child, watching for signs of awakening in his heart and spirit. We ought to practice this art above all, of course, with our own grandchildren, but other children, too, ought to share this love. What otherwise do they mean when they call an old person grand-dad or granny?

Warm yourself, old man, in the brand-new sun of childhood, and may your evening sun shed its rays on the child!

Mother Michel's Cat

I have never much liked the song about Mother Michel's cat, which grownups, heaven knows why, make children learn. I have always liked cats, so I could easily understand why she was unhappy calling her lost pussy through the open window and wearing, I always imagined, a loose smock and a white cap on her head. And as for Father Lustucru, well, he never meant anything to me. Sometimes I thought that he may have captured the tom-cat while he was out walking and secretly eaten it. At other times, I imagined that he had killed it in order to be able to take its place in the affection of his neighbor, Mother Michel, and at the same time get his hands on her money. The poor old woman was alone in the world and she needed a tom-cat to keep her company. The animal gave her a chance to pour out all the love that her old heart contained.

After all, domestic animals are like children—they like old people, and for the same reason that children like them. And old people like animals. They have reserves of gentleness and patience which dogs and cats sense. Dogs and cats are perceptive animals. Old people hardly ever play with their pets, as they undoubtedly did when they were children, or as they may perhaps have done in maturer years, so long as they stayed young in heart. But they do not treat them roughly. They fondle them affectionately. Whenever they can, they take their dog for a walk or converse intimately with their cat.

I remember my grandfather's dog very well. He was a little Pomeranian with the not uncommon name of Kiki. There are very few of them about now, with their sharp muzzles, pointed ears, wicked little eyes, and tails resembling a plume of feathers or a trumpet. Like all such little creatures, he was by nature a bit snappy and quick-tempered. He reserved all his affection for my grandfather, whom he followed everywhere, and for my grandmother, whom he would fetch to the door when anyone rang by tugging at her apron. When he died, it happened quite suddenly. In a matter of moments, he passed from quivering life to a corpse-like stiffness. My grandfather did not say a word. But he never replaced him with another pet. He did not want to expose himself to further suffering.

I think it is true to say that a child's education is not complete without the friendship of animals. I also think that old people should also be able to enjoy this friendship, even if they do not live entirely alone, because they need a being that is always there, ready to love them and be quite dependent on them. Rational middle-aged people do not understand this friendship between the old man and his pet. I have often heard ladies who do charitable or social work criticizing old people who have barely enough to live on, yet insist on keeping their dog or their cat. It is not that they are more unfeeling than other people—it is just that they do not understand, that is all. And I know plenty of people who can hardly suppress a smile—and some who laugh aloud—when they hear an old lady they are taking to an old people's home asking what will happen to her cat. Poor Mother Michel—mocked eternally by Father Lustucru!

Of course, friendship for a pet should not degenerate into a ridiculous form of sentimentality. I don't know which is the more irritating of the two beings—the "little doggy-wog with his mummykins" or the "mummykins with her little doggy-wog." But even such excesses can be forgiven, if we know that behind them are frustrated feelings.

I cannot forget what a source of happiness a loving pet can be for an old man or woman and I would like younger people of all ages to remember not to make all too easy jokes about it, since those jokes are not always funny and often cruel.

Philemon and Baucis

Love is another positive value of old age. By this I mean love in the original and precise sense of the word. Not simply love in general, the love that we call charity, but love between man and woman.

In the book from which I have already quoted, Simone de Beauvoir had some very distressing and unsavory things to say about the sex life of old people. Her aim was clearly to prove that they could—and, although she did not say so explicitly, must—continue with their sexual activities. To support this argument, she provided a certain amount of rather disgusting evidence. Anyone who wanted to be really cruel would say that she was looking into her own future and trying to find some consolation in the pitiless advance of old age. We get older, of course, and we have to die, but we should be able to experience enjoyment until the end.

What does it matter to me that Victor Hugo was still able to indulge in sexual exploits when he was more than eighty and that he entered the cost of these adventures in his account book under the word "charities." This knowledge does not in any way lessen my admiration for him as a poet, even though it certainly does not increase my regard for him as a man. I could guess at these exploits from reading his *Songs of the Streets and the Woods* and did not really want to know any more precise details.

It is common knowledge that there are many old rams—in the picturesque slang of pre-1914 France, we called them "old walkers" no doubt because they were always prowling about looking for women—and ancient nymphs who may not, it is true, be nymphomaniacs, but who are certainly no longer young and beautiful goddesses of the woods and streams. These elderly coquettes have to put up, as a substitute for love, with well-dressed young men who were, when I was young, and are still, I believe, known as gigolos.

What does all this prove? The old Greeks and Romans were right to be ashamed of these amorous adventures of old age—*turpe senilis amor*—because, after all, they can never be any more than parodies of love. The two old men who surprised Susanna bathing may have worn majestic beards, but that was the only majesty they could claim! Love and youth go together—they are both flowers of the same springtime.

Are we to believe that we are delivered from all the temptations of the flesh when we are old? This was often thought to be the case in the past, and men were glad of it. One Greek dramatist gave thanks to the gods because old age would in the end spare him those thoughts and temptations that he believed were shameful. Unfortunately, reality is not quite as simple as that. According to at least one saint, some temptations do not disappear until a little while after death. Old age calms down the passions of the flesh, but calming down is not the same as ending. Here too, old age is what it has been made by youth and middle age. The man who has been all his life in the habit of controlling his passions will continue to do so, but the man who has not will continue on his downward path.

I am not thinking of this when I call love a positive value of old age. It is, after all, not the kind of love that we have been considering that binds together the old couples whom I find so admirable. When they were young, their love began in an encounter of the flesh and the spirit, *eros* and *agape* in the language of the Greeks. With the passage of time, *eros* gradually receded into the background until it disappeared before *agape,* love of the flesh before love of the spirit. This does not in any way mean that their love ceased at any time to be an authentic experience of the way the two sexes complement each other. You sometimes hear it said that love changes into friendship in old age, but I think that this is not quite true. Love continues to be love, since the memory of total unity cannot be effaced. But sexuality is not essential to love in old age. Old people may not come together bodily, but their souls remain united, at least according to the old song, by "a golden chain that is only broken at death." I have even known couples bound together so strongly by that chain that, when one died, the other could no longer resist. They lived together and died together. Immortal chains bound mortal bodies! We should not, moreover, think that such closely united couples are so uncommon. They are often very humble, simple, and good people who were incapable of expressing their love in concepts or words. They just loved each other! And God, whom they loved in their love for each other, gave them this great gift. Their death proved that love is stronger than death.

I hope no one will criticize me for being naively optimistic and seeing everything through rose colored spectacles. I have lived a long time and seen life close up. I don't think I am guilty of optimism based on illusion. What is more, a glance at one or two of Courteline's quick sketches would be enough to convince me to the contrary. You don't have to tell me about those old couples who are so indifferent to each other that they live in total solitude side by side, those who can only put up with the constant quarrelling that is habitual in marriage by force of habit or those whose marriage has never been more than the juxtaposition of two selfish beings. Such marriages exist, but they are extreme examples. There are many others that still contain certain elements of love, but are characterized by an atmosphere of constant nagging, grumbling, and scolding. There are so many aged households in which the storm never breaks, but where the rain is always falling and the sky is grey—like the proverbial married couple, both of whom worked in the same silk spinning mill in Lyon. Each of these two "bobbins," as employees in the silk industry were called then, accused the other of constantly finding fault—and both were right.

All this is, alas, only too true—just as the other cases of eternal love that I have mentioned are also true. The fact remains that, despite all imperfections, mediocrity, and changes for the worse in mind and body, in old age man continues to be man and woman continues to be woman. They go on being different from, complementary to, and in need of each other. The fire of love may burn less brightly and it may even be reduced to no more than a spark, but it never goes out completely, at least as long as the couple take the trouble to keep it alive by attending to it together. For some couples, love is never more than a flash in the pan, a sudden sensual blaze that passes very quickly. In old age, the relationship between such couples is cold and habitual. Others, however, have throughout marriage fanned the flame of their poor love by giving themselves to each other again and again. Their love lasts in time and eternity.

There was an ironical and yet tender song composed, I think, by Désaugiers, in which an old couple, Monsieur and Madame Denis, sang a duet:

Why do you not last for ever,
fire of our younger years?

Well, the very fact that they were both asking this question in their old, cracked voices shows that the fire of love was not yet out, even though Monsieur Denis wore false teeth and Madame Denis wore a wig.

Roundabout the beginning of this century, Christians rediscovered the nobility of the flesh and the greatness of human love. This made them praise and venerate young married couples, sometimes with an almost childish sentimentality. They evolved an entire spirituality based on the honeymoon, with the idea of extending it eternally and excluding any possible occurrence of a withering April moon. Dare I say that the example of old, loving married couples bears more convincing witness to love?

You old couples who are left alone in your silent, empty houses, from which your children have flown one by one to follow their own lives—you should be aware of your good fortune and recognize that even death will not destroy it, since, however abandoned you may be by time, eternity is yours. Sing a hymn of thanksgiving to the God of love! And you old people who have been left quite alone—turn both to the past, while you are still able to do it, and cherish the memory, which is irreplaceable and unfading, of having loved and of having been loved and also to the future—to the eternity of God where you will rediscover your love, made young again, in the immortal youth of God's love.

This married love has been expressed in the beautiful myth of Philemon and Baucis. Those two old people had given hospitality to Zeus, when he visited them in the disguise of a traveler. He wanted to reward them by a gift of their own choosing. They asked him to immortalize their love. Not even

Zeus was able to prevent men and women from dying, but he metamorphosed them into trees, the long life of which in this world is an image of eternity. Baucis, it is said, became a lime tree and Philemon an oak.

Both stood side by side, their foliage intermingling, for centuries. The God of life and love fulfills love's hope of immortality, as glimpsed in Greek mythology, by the resurrection of the body. Your love will not vanish—eternity lies ahead of it.

The Oak and the Lime Tree

Fine, delicate, and sweetly scented, the lime tree is the woman.
It has strength but is strong in a peaceful and gentle way
without effort.
Knotty and hard, imposing its authority on all that grows around it, the oak is the man.
Buttressed on its roots, spreading out its crenated leaves, it
asserts its presence.
The oak and the lime tree have grown side by side in the same earth.
They have matured slowly together under the same sun and the same rain.
They have stood up to the same storms.
The oak has breathed the scent of the lime tree.
The lime tree has relied on the strength of the oak.
And now they are both old—their trunks are hollow, their branches breaking.
One day the lightning will strike them, or the woodcutter will fell them,
or time will wear them down
and they will mingle with the earth from which they first emerged.

But, in their old age, their branches are still intertwined
and the traveler rests in the shade of their leaves,
under the scent of the lime tree, the strength of the oak and their
overlapping shadows.
The oak and the lime tree—they represent you, old couples, united
forever in love.
You have grown up together and fought side by side. Your seed has
fallen into the ground that feeds it.
Both of you will die and that is right, because the oak cannot live
without the lime tree, or the lime without the oak.
But under God's sun, there is an eternal garden of living water
and green growth
where your branches, oak and lime tree, will be entwined forever
under the light of love.

Old Wines and Old Friends

Very few things are improved by age. According to folk wisdom, there are only two—wine and friendship. Folk wisdom is right about this. Everyone would agree that all wines are made better with the passing of time. We ought also to agree that it is the same with friendships. Just think for a moment! One of the finest rays of the evening sun is that we have the leisure to savor old friendships as we taste old wines. We have none of the illusions, and we make none of the mistakes of youth in evaluating friendship, nor are we in a hurry or overanxious as we are in middle age, when we have to pass friendship by.

A friendship that has stood the test of time, separations, contradictions, and opposing forces shows by the very fact of its survival that it is true. Such friendships exist in many different forms. Some, though not very many, go back to childhood and even to early childhood, to the time when mothers visited each other with their little children or to schooldays. Others originate during shared ordeals such as war. Many are based on interests in common and on similar temperaments, while some have just the opposite cause—quite different or even radically opposed attitudes to life have been known to unite people in close friendship. Some friendships continue without a check throughout the lives of both friends, whereas others are interrupted for long periods, yet, as soon as the friends meet again, they find each other just as they were before the apparent break and continue the discussion that they had left off, so it seems, the day before. It hardly matters really. What matters is that there are friendships.

Should we be happy to have only a few friends? Perhaps we should, at least as a general rule. True friends are certainly not plentiful. The poet La Fontaine wrote:

> Two true friends lived in Monomotapa,

indicating how rare friendship is by using such a bizarre name for a distant and legendary country. But there are, of course, exceptions to the general rule. Some people have such a gift for friendship that they live and die surrounded by countless true friends. I would not hesitate to say that, in the interchange of friendship, such men usually give much more than they receive. But once again, it hardly matters. All that matters is the friendship or friendships.

I have often said, written or sung these words: "Drinking a bottle of good old wine with good old friends," because there is something in them that I cannot define that enchants me. The enchantment of these words began when I was very young and age has only increased the spell they have over me. I can so easily think of friends sitting together in the winter beside the fire, sipping Beaujolais that has been brought up to the temperature of the room, or under the trees in the summer drinking iced white wine, smoking their pipes and speaking very little and without haste, exchanging old memories. May the Lord give us many such meetings with our friends! They are oases in the desert that we cross in the pilgrimage of our lives.

But why have I not said anything about old friends who are women? There are, after all, women whom we have not loved, but with whom we have enjoyed a peaceful and lasting understanding. There was no question here of a male type of friendship, rough, easy going, back-slapping, and perhaps a bit boastful. Our relationship was always more delicate and tender. But it was still friendship and a genuine ray of the evening sun.

Death, with his scythe, cuts down one after another of our old friends, casting a dark shadow over our old age. The loss of friends is surely one of the greatest sorrows of increasing years. But, on the other hand, one of the purest joys as we get older is the constancy of old friendships.

Old wines and old friends. . . . When I was a boy, I knew two old retired men—two friends—who lived in the same village. One of them was completely deaf and his handicap made all communication almost impossible. Yet these two friends visited each other regularly and spent hours together, smoking their pipes, drinking the local wine, and not speaking a word to each other. I used to wonder what pleasure they found in each other's company. But since growing up I have begun to understand. The mere presence of the other enabled friendship to be expressed and, as both were Christians, God was also present in their presence with each other.

My Old Friend

When I call you my old friend, I am not just using, quite unthinkingly, a ready-made expression.
No, you really are my old friend—our friendship has lasted for more than forty years.
And I am your old friend, too, because of the same friendship.
And we know that we are friends until the end of the road.
We met when we were very young and the whole of life was ahead of us, like a beautiful fruit seen in the distance.
We do not resemble each other in any way, either in appearance or in our characters or ideas—our ideas are often quite different!
But, when we were young, we loved life, and we also wanted to love Christ.
A spark appeared between us and set light to a flame that has never gone out.
So we walked along the road together, behind Saint Francis and behind Christ.
We went through rain and good weather together, through cold and heat and through pain and joy.
We fought together for the same causes, confronted the same dangers and shared the same hopes.
Together, my old friend.

My Old Friend

And now we are both old. Life is behind us like a beautiful fruit
that we have not been able to pick.
When we look back, we can see the long way that we have
come.
In front of us, only a short stretch of road is left.
But we cannot forget this long way that we have covered
together and the short stretch of road that is left—we shall
cover it together.

It does not matter very much if old age makes our legs weak
and our breath short.
Our friendship is as young as it was forty years ago,
Even when we are separated by a great distance, we know we
are still together.
And when we meet again, we are still the same.
My old friend.

My old friend, let us go on to meet death.
And let the first one to arrive wait for the other in the eternity
of God.

Solitude

But there are old people who have no family and no friends. They either never had children or else they have lost them. They have spent their lives in a very restricted environment, and the few friends they had have disappeared one after the other. Some of these old people are in this position because they have led closed and selfish lives—having children and friends is a preparation for old age. They reap what they have sown—nothing. But this is not the time to take them to task. We should be sorry for them. Other old people, of course, are alone because of misfortune. They may have had too few relatives or they may have lived too long. And then there are those old men and women who are the victims of ingratitude—deserted by their children and left in the unhappiest situation of all.

All these old people have only solitude as their companion. No one is there to look after them, help them, or even to listen to them. They are alone in their empty rooms, which echo weakly to their steps, and in homes for the aged and even hospitals. There are so many of them! Great numbers, but each one alone. To overcome loneliness, all you need are a few neighbors, a pack of cards, or some wool and needles. While you are playing or knitting, the stories of other neighbors or old friends go the rounds. Even in quite comfortable homes, how many old people there are who are enclosed in solitude because they are deaf. Deafness is surely one of the greatest misfortunes of old age, and modern medicine can still do almost nothing to overcome it.

We ought also to be very grateful to all those who are attempting to deal with the problems of isolation in old age—by providing clubs and by visiting old people's homes. Young people visit the aged in their homes and so do the brothers of Saint Vincent de Paul as well as many other groups. These are all excellent attempts, but they are not made in every town and every district and it cannot be denied that, in the end, they are really no more than palliatives—rather like those tranquillizers that make it easier for you to go to sleep. For this is, after all, the great modern problem! We extend life without knowing what to do with it afterwards.

I think a good deal about you, lonely old people, and with great compassion. It is not difficult for me to feel compassionate, because I am fast approaching the time when your fate will possibly be my own. Writers and men of action also become victims of solitude. If they live far beyond the period of their greatest activity, the contrast between their popularity then and their present condition makes life very hard indeed in old age. I have so often seen the face of a long forgotten "star" of the past light up with happiness when he happened to meet someone who remembered him in his heyday or who at least had heard of him by reputation! One in particular whom I recall vividly—that old Montmartre singer to whom I sang one of his own songs which was famous in its day, but which he himself could not remember properly. I had been taught it when I was a child. I was one of the few people of my own generation who knew it.

Solitude brings melancholy in its wake, and there is no remedy for these evils so long as we live only in time. The only ones to escape from them are those who believe firmly in eternity, because such people are never really alone and they are never permanently imprisoned by the sadness of being abandoned. They know that there is one who will never forget them and who is always present in front of them, beside them, and in their hearts. In his agony, Christ experienced not only solitude, but also the pangs of complete dereliction. "Whoever follows me will not walk in darkness." Whoever lives with me will never be alone. Our great friend in the morning of our lives, Christ, is now our companion in the evening of life, and we discover his presence in prayer. "He looks at me and I look at him" was what the old peasant of Ars, silent in front of the tabernacle, told his parish priest.

O Christ, I place in your care all solitary old people, all hermits despite themselves even when they are in a crowd. May their solitude be united with yours!

Sickness

All old age, even the most healthy and vigorous, seems in a sense to be like a sickness and, what is more, a sickness from which we die. Most old people suffer from some of these major or minor disorders resulting from the imperfect functioning of worn out organs that cannot be replaced like the parts of a car. We simply have to put up with them with courage and good humor, at least so long as they are not too severe. My rheumatism, for example, has one advantage—it provides me with a free, portable barometer! And if I am condemned by the medical profession to follow a strict diet, as I have been at times, I do it in the knowledge that I would never have been able to lead such an ascetic and disciplined life simply by exerting my own will power.

I am not thinking now, however, of the inevitable effects of the aging process—those many wheels that have become rusty and seized up—but of real sickness, the serious type of disease that keeps you in bed or in your armchair and is not improved by pills, injections, or other cures. I am thinking, for example, of paralysis or those terrible difficulties in movement and speech that result from hemiplegia. And then there are those many heart diseases that force you to live in the shadow of death, but at the same time surround you with so many precautions that the death which continues to hang over you like a dark threat may even in the long run seem like liberation. These are among the many miseries of the body which make us not only permanently preoccupied with our health, but also even permanently bedridden.

Sickness of this kind does not, however, always mean intolerable and continuous suffering. The sick person may go from crisis to crisis, with intervals of well-being and the violence of the bad periods may make him appreciate the periods of calm. He may not even suffer at all physically. For any sufficiently lucid old person, however, the moral suffering can be very severe. "Look what has become of me!" one of my ex-teachers said to me once. He had been so intelligent, but his mind was going in bits and pieces and he still had enough understanding of himself to be aware of it. "Look what has become of me!" I could not help thinking then that I, too, might one day experience that same gradual and inexorable loss of mental power, that same decline, not into death that would set me free, but into an abyss where I would go on living an obscure and almost vegetable existence.

The worst suffering experienced by those men and women who can remember how strong they were and how others were dependent on them before they became chronically sick is their sense of permanent humiliation. To become no more than a limp rag, unable to do anything for oneself, forced to rely again and again on other people even for the must trivial or intimate needs, treated perhaps in a jovial and slightly domineering way or else like a baby and sometimes neglected or pushed about by people doing the job for the pay—this is surely humiliating in the extreme! No wonder many old people in that state might long for death if, by that strange inner contradiction of human nature, they did not become all the more firmly attached to life the lower the flame flickered, clinging on all the more desperately, despite their infirmities, as it burnt down to the point of extinction.

Louis Veuillot, I recall, asked God to let him die while he was still quite fit and to spare him the weeping of women, the bearers of what he called, with the characteristic euphemism of the period, "ridiculous vases." His words certainly do not bear witness to a heroic Christian faith—the Christian has to accept God's will as to the hour and the manner of his death. But I must admit that I can understand Louis Veuillot here. If I had the choice, I would prefer to die upright, still serving, and not bedridden, lingering on, as so many sick old people I have known, for months or even years, halfway between life and death.

Poor old man, your mind and body laid waste by sickness, my poor, afflicted, worn down and humiliated brother—how absurd and futile it is for me to sit here with you and say consoling words that cost me no more than the trouble to say them, while assuming that good natured, condescending, and cheerful manner that all those who are well seem to adopt when they visit the sick. "Well, grand-dad, how are things today? Not too good? . . . Cheer up! You'll feel better tomorrow. . . ." I can only suffer with you, without speaking, be sympathetic in the literal sense of the word. Maybe that silent compassion will lighten your burden just a little.

I have spoken about solitude. All sickness is solitude. It is all the more lonely for the old man or woman, who is already solitary because of old age, even when he or she is surrounded by affection, which may be too demonstrative or perhaps a bit tyrannical. Sick old man, my brother, you are alone, despite my presence at your bedside.

And yet you are not alone. You do not suffer alone, because you are suffering with Christ on the cross. Your suffering is not useless because, united with the passion of Christ, it is helping to save the world. There was a time when you used to follow Christ in your activity. Now you follow him in your immobility.

You may not have the strength to pray, but you can still pray just by thinking of Christ suffering and saving. It is fashionable these days for "emancipated" Christians to laugh about the rosary. But it is, in my experience, the only possible form of prayer for the sick and the dying. It is a prayer that need not be enunciated in words. It can be expressed simply by the twitching of your fingers on the beads. It is your prayer, my brother, when you are overwhelmed by sickness.

The Sacrament of the Sick

The Church provides the sacrament of the sick to strengthen the bodies and souls of those who are suffering. The oil of the sacrament is like that used on the body of an athlete to make it soft and supple for the combat. The spirit of the sacrament of the sick was called extreme unction and was indeed a last oiling, a final laying out before death. Believers were either ignorant of its true nature or else afraid. The result was that the sacrament was often put off until the last moments of life, when the person was in a coma or even when he was breathing his last.

Fortunately, we have at last rediscovered the simple fact that the sacrament of the sick is not to be confused with what was known in conventional language as the last sacraments. "Fortified by the last rites of the Church" were words which often appeared on announcements of a person's decease or those familiar black-edged cards. They often meant conditional absolution or extreme unction administered during the haze of that person's last agony.

In reaction to this, we may, of course, be going too far in the opposite direction today. I am not at all sure that it is right to give the sacrament of the sick in public in a church to old people whose health is good, on the pretext that they are candidates for death. That death may not, after all, happen for years.

Is it foolish of me to think that the sacrament of the sick is for the sick and not only for those who are at death's door, but also not for those who are getting on all right, even though they may be getting on in years?

And is it tactless of me to believe that the sacrament of the sick, with the physical contact and the oiling that it involves, ought to take place in a sphere of intimacy, within the circle of those who have cared for the sick person, the family and, if there are any, the friends?

I admit that great old age is a kind of sickness, of which a person may die at any moment, very gently, like a flame going out, to use the familiar image. But that is a specific case.

The fact remains that the sacrament of the sick is, as Monsieur de La Palisse would say, for the sick, whether death is watching over them or not. It is not exclusively intended to prepare those who are dying for their long journey into the next world. It is above all meant to give sick people the strength and the courage to carry the cross of their illness.

You don't die from it! The proof of this is that Monsieur Jacques Duclos, the communist leader, has received it and indeed boasted about it on television during an election campaign. On the contrary, you live because of it, as it gives you back your taste for life.

My good, sick old brothers—insist on your right to receive this sacrament. It is yours, even though some priests are nowadays in no hurry to climb up the stairs to administer it to you. The holy oil will flow over your limbs and the whole Church will be praying for and with you, while the two candles are burning, one on each side of the crucifix to which the one who has healed us by his suffering is forever nailed.

Our Sister Death

We know, of course, that the end of old age, the last end, is death. We cannot hide this from ourselves, even if we are so passionately attached to life that all thought of death is far from our minds and even if the death of others is not enough to make us think of our own. It is no good behaving like an ostrich! How disappointing it is to hide the fact of his imminent death from the sick person, when he is all the time aware of it himself! And how foolish it is for him not to speak about his death for fear of saddening those around him, who are, in turn, equally foolishly, pretending in a clumsy way to hope for his recovery because they are afraid of frightening him! Such a silent drama has all the attributes of a tragicomedy. No one is deceived by such an exchange of pious lies.

It was, I believe, La Rochefoucauld who said: "It is not possible to look at the face of the sun or of death." This strikes one at first as a very profound thought, but it is not true. You can look at the sun through smoked glasses, and you do not need the eye of an eagle to look at death. During the war, I more than once waited for a dying man to slip away at the last moment into death. Why should I be less able to do the same in old age?

Old age is the anteroom in which we wait for death. We may have to sit there for a short time or for a long time, as we do in the doctor's waiting room. But we can be quite sure that sooner or later death will open the door and beckon us. Whether we are ready or not, we shall have to respond to that call.

It makes me sad to think that present-day Christians, who are, of course, children of a century which has carried fear of death to the extreme limit, so that it has become almost a phobia, can themselves no longer think of death and dying and have left it to atheistic existentialists to formulate a philosophy of death. That great writer, André Malraux, was obsessed with death and the thought runs through all his books. In a sense, his greatness comes from his preoccupation with this fact. I know that Malraux was not really an existentialist and that he was, at the deepest level of his being, probably not even sure whether he was an atheist. But it is not possible to call him a Christian, whereas it is quite certain that he was an excellent representative of a spiritual and intellectual trend that has dominated the twentieth century and that he expressed a desire for a death that would give meaning to life.

There have, of course, been times when Christians thought perhaps too much about death. We only have to recall those sinister and macabre representations of a grinning skeleton leading in a grim dance people of all ages and conditions, from king to beggar.

> When I think of all those skulls
> piled up in charnel-houses—
> they were once all privy councillors,
> porters, bishops, or lamplighters.

I am very fond indeed of Villon and Holbein. But was their view of death really Christian? And those sermons about death which were given to children at the time of their first communion, filling them with terrifying dreams, or Wesley's preaching that reduced the crowds who heard them almost to an epileptic frenzy! How much calmer, more gentle, more filled with hope and more Christian was the traditional Mass of the Dead, before the introduction of that flaming meteorite, the *Dies Irae*! When I was younger, the brothers of the Good Death used to sit in the choir-stalls holding professional candle-holders, each one with a plaque showing a black and white skull above two crossed thigh bones!

In those days, Christians were so bowed down with the thought of death that they hardly found time to live. Life was an anticipation of death. There were so many hymns, when I was young, emphasizing death. I well remember singing, in my clear soprano voice and with very little understanding of the words:

> All will end, o sinners, at death, at death!

or

> Our life is but a brief shadow!
> We are born only to die!

or

> Death is already at my heels—
> O sad night—and approaching fast!

I remember liking the last hymn, because it danced and leapt along.

This preoccupation with death was often accompanied by a fear of hell—the result of countless "hell-fire" sermons. We were not spared a single punishment if it affected our sense of sight, hearing, smell, taste, or touch. All that the preachers of that time forgot to do was to impress on us the real suffering of damnation—that we might be eternally separated from God and have to live without him. Surely that is the essential pain of hell! In his semi-autobiographical novel, *A Portrait of the Artist,* James Joyce provides a vivid hell-fire sermon which obviously had a deep effect on the young author. From the time that I began to listen to sermons, I must have heard that sermon or one very similar to it at least a dozen times. In it, God appeared as a cruel and arbitrary despot waiting for us to die in order to cast us into the eternal fire.

I do not regret that period of Christianity or that kind of spirituality which inspired Ingmar Bergman's great film *The Seventh Seal*—a disturbing vision of Europe at the time of the Hundred Years' War and the Black Death. What I really regret is that Christians, in going from one extreme to the other, would seem to want to forget a death that will not forget them.

Certainly the thought of death is not amusing. You cannot laugh if you look in the mirror and see, reflected in it, a skeleton—as in a number of old legends. Yet we read in Scripture—at least in the Vulgate—that the strong Woman will laugh on the last day. And I have seen men and women die, slowly, or suddenly, and violently, with a smile on their lips—almost, you might say, with a rose in their mouths.

I have made a distinction between slow and violent death. It is, of course, an artificial distinction, because all death is violent. The separation of the soul from the body is against nature, since man wants to know and love in soul and body. Death does violence to man's deep wish in his innermost being to continue to be and to his human desire to live forever. As Christians, we know the reason for this violence. Death is, after all, the wages of sin and the result of the disorder into which man and his world were thrown by that first fall of which we are aware but which we cannot explain. Death is a disorder in the harmony of creation, and we continue to suffer from it as we suffer from all disorder. Even if we are no longer obsessed, as man was in the past, by death, we still have to recognize it and understand it. It is not amusing to die.

Even if we know that God's infinite justice is also his infinite mercy and that the two are inseparably bound together, it will not be amusing to stand in front of him. Yet appearing before him will not be like appearing in front of a human judge, since God does not judge us from the outside—we judge ourselves in front of God.... As soon as we have, however obscurely and confusedly, perceived that it is God and recognized what we are, all that we shall feel will be a holy fear. It is terrible to fall into the hands of the living God, Scripture tells us. There will be, on one side, God—all purity, all goodness, omnipotent, Being itself in infinite splendor—and, on the other, us—almost nothing, weak, ephemeral, sinners covered with dust and ashes. We are drawn toward him with a force which we cannot resist and which comes from the center of our being, but the great weight of earth that fills us holds us back and drives us, like Marlowe's Faustus, to implore the mountains to fall on us so that we shall be hidden from that love which is as violent as fire and as pure as ice and of which we are so unworthy. This tension between what is pulling us toward God and what is holding us back from God is perhaps what we call purgatory. We have to pass through that burning pit in order to be made pure and worthy to love that Love whom we did not love when he humbly appealed to us to love him through the medium of our brothers. O blood of Christ, pour down on us and wash us clean!

This fear of God should not, however, sink to the level of a servile terror. We should never be afraid of God in that way, because he is good, because he loves us, and because he wants us to be the brothers of Christ, who was God and man. Nor should we be afraid of death, because this final passing—our passing away and the passing of time into eternity—takes us at once to God's love.

I think that Francis of Assisi said everything that a Christian could say about death when he spoke of our sister bodily death in his Canticle of the Creatures. Although death was introduced into the world by our sin, it is, like life, God's servant. So we have our sister life and our sister death.

Sister death is as old as time, yet always young. She takes us in her arms to God. She is both hard and gentle, hard, we may say, because she is gentle. She makes us suffer in order to give us eternal happiness.

The Christian cannot think of death as a final shipwreck, the breaking up of all life. It is quite the opposite. It is a fulfillment, bringing with it the fullness of maturity. If it is an end, this should be understood not in the sense of finishing, but as the reaching of a goal after a long, patient search. Death sums up our life and gives it its full meaning.

This end is also a beginning. In the old preface of a Mass for the dead, we used to sing: Vita mutatur non tollitur. Death changes life; it does not take it away. It changes life by raising it above time into eternity. It makes us pass from life in time to eternal life. Or rather, it is as if it breaks a very thin skin and gives us access to that eternal life that has always been in us, thanks to God's grace. It closes our eyes of flesh and directs our gaze to God's eternity.

This is why—and I not only repeat what I have already said, but insist on it—we must never be afraid of death, but look forward to it as the fulfillment of a hope. When the door of the anteroom opens, we shall not see the old man with a scythe and an hourglass emerge, but our good and lovely sister, dressed in white and crowned with a garland of flowers.

So let us wait calmly, patiently, and without fear for death. I do not think that those old men and women who claim that they are praying fervently for death to come quickly are really sincere in their supplications. The old fable of La Fontaine about the woodcutter and death, which goes back to a very remote theme in folklore, shows how vain such appeals are. The poor woodcutter, "covered with green boughs," overworked and burdened with taxes, calls on death to set him free, but, as soon as death comes in answer to his call, he hastens to ask something quite different: that death should go away as quickly as possible.

I have seen that fable enacted before my eyes! An old lady who had as much to complain about as anyone else, but no more than others was always wearying death with the same demand: "Oh when will God take me? I am suffering so much! What can I do if I go on living?" One day, she became really ill and was in danger of dying. At once her tune changed: "Oh God, I am dying! Have mercy on me! Spare me!" Death heard her plea and she lived for many years. But she had learned her lesson and never again prayed to die.

I know that old people commit suicide and that there are more of them than is ever said or that most of us think. But, in most cases, the instinct to live is stronger than what Freud called the instinct to die—a term which I have always found very debatable. If you value life at all, it is surely futile and ridiculous to beckon to a death that you do not want. As for me, I must confess that I am like La Fontaine's old woman:

> The further the old woman went,
> the more she learnt
> and the less she wanted to die.

I know that I shall eventually learn everything at once in God's light, but in the meantime I still have much to learn in the light of the sun here on earth!

I have already said what we have to think about death, but I want to say it again here, because we shall never know the hour or the manner of our death and it would be absurd and unnecessary to let our minds be filled with all kinds of gloomy fantasies. The person who is terrified of dying of cancer is run over by a bus. The one who hopes to die suddenly in fact dies calmly in his bed without even knowing he is dying. Death is like war—it is impossible to know today what will happen to us tomorrow. I have on several occasions been in situations which seemed certain to end in death, yet here I am—still alive! I well remember that enormous land mine that blew up during an air raid only a few yards away from me. But when it fell, it was kind enough to do so in a sunken road with high embankments in which the blast was lost and the fragments were buried. I needed a few moments to convince myself that I was still alive. Since that day, I have never again been afraid of death. Am I being fatalistic? No—it is simply a question of acceptance.

I have just said it again—acceptance. But it is, after all, a keyword. So let us really accept death as an integral part of the human condition and therefore also as the expression of God's will.

At the same time, let us also accept the uncertainty that surrounds death: "Watch, therefore, for you know neither the day nor the hour!" It is true—we shall never know when the master will come back, in what quiet hour of the night. "Blessed are those servants whom he finds awake when he comes!" Let us stay awake, then, and wait for him, in the knowledge that old age is the last part of our vigil. The Lord will come back and he will come back very soon. It may be within thirty days, thirty months, or thirty years—it is all the same compared with eternity. Lord, I am awake, watching and waiting, like the almond tree, that vigilant tree, waiting for the first days of spring in order to put out its flowers.

Watching and waiting is being ready. The keyword, acceptance, goes together with another: preparation. This word may at first call sad images of mourning to mind, but preparing oneself for death should not consist of gloomy meditations or an anticipation of death by adopting a graveyard attitude. I am not saying that those hermits who used to spend their lives praying in front of a human skull were wrong, but I would certainly say that it is not absolutely necessary to have a human skull in front of you when you are getting ready to die.

No, preparing to die is living intensely, as God wants us to live! It is growing old beautifully, as God wants us to grow old. It is ending our lives by giving them a meaning to which death will add a final, definitive, and full conclusion. It is watching and waiting, in other words, thinking and acting all the time as though the Lord were going to knock on our door at any moment. It is, as Aloysius Gonzaga said (and Charles Péguy was enchanted with the saying), simply playing ball. Jesuit novices were addicted to playing ball in the sixteenth century, but they had to stop quite often to take part in what used to be called "edifying" discussions. "If we were told that we would all die in an hour's time, what would you do?" Each novice had his own solution, and each competed with the others to find the most pious answer. When Aloysius was asked what he would do, he surprised everyone by saying simply: "I would just go on playing ball."

It does not much matter whether it is true or not. The meaning of the anecdote is very profound. It shows above all that the young Aloysius, who died when he was twenty-three, had understood both life and death and that, despite all appearances, there is no discontinuity between them.

Play ball, then, or checkers, or dominoes, or whatever you like! In other words, gentlemen, go on smoking your pipe and looking at your roses! Go on serving others and praying when you have to! And you, ladies—go on knitting and cooking good meals if possible—and serving others and praying when you have to!

Death and the Cross

O death, daughter of sin, you were the enemy of the whole human race—and my enemy.
You were the close companion of the Prince of death, the fearful rider who, together with the Devil, followed the horseman.
You were the queen of terror and the last agony,
the handmaid of the void,
the dark angel of eternal night
and the gloomy, inevitable reef on which every human adventure was wrecked.
Your shears were inexorable and cut through the thread of every life.
Skeleton with a sunken nose—your scythe severed all loves and all friendships.
You were not even useful in adding piquancy to man's pleasures:
"Let us eat and drink and be merry, for tomorrow we die!"
O death, you took your victims away in your ghostly chariot to unknown shadows.

But Christ came.
He conquered you, death, by his own death on the cross.
He went down into the realm of the dead, bringing his light.

He rose again on Easter morning so that his Resurrection
would also be ours.
O death, you are no longer the daughter of sin, but God's
creature,
our sister bodily death—we cannot resist you, but we are sorry
for you.
My sister death—I am waiting for you, without impatience but
also without fear.
You will come at the hour appointed by God, whose punctual
servant you are.
You will close my eyes both to the beauty of the world and to its
ugliness and misery.
You will entrust my body to the earth, where the bodies of my
ancestors were laid to rest.
You will take my soul to the love of the Lord.
You, my dear sister death, will let me enter eternal rest, where
I shall be in the coolness of flowing water and endless light.
You, my pure sister death, will give me the peace that I have
sought all my life without ever finding it.

O my sister bodily death, it is easy to wait for you.
It is easy to welcome you and to be carried by you.
You will bear us up while we are waiting for the day of the
Lord,
when we shall once again find our bodies of flesh, transfigured,
when time and death, God's creatures, will come to an end
and when you will be no more than a memory in the great life
of God.

Life Ascending

Death blots out the evening sun, but replaces it with the sun of eternity whose light never fades. Death is not an endless night. It is unchanging light. Despite all the agonies that surround it, then, it is the happy end of a pilgrimage.

It is not a new idea in spiritual writing to compare life with a pilgrimage. It is as old as spiritual literature itself, but its age does not make it any less relevant to us today. Man is essentially a traveler. He is *homo viator,* traveling through time. The Christian sees this journey as a pilgrimage, a continuous journey toward a divine end. The whole of mankind is going on a pilgrimage through time, passing on its way through many cities and civilizations.

One of the great Christian paradoxes is that man, who tills the soil and builds cities, must go on planting and building as though he were to be settled forever, yet at the same time he is always conscious that he and the world that he creates are passing, that he is a pilgrim with no permanent dwelling place and that his human condition is that of a traveler.

He is most sharply aware of this apparent contradiction when he is old. We old people have not in any sense finished our work. We go on planting and building to provide food and shelter for those who follow us. But we feel that our time is limited and that our work is always exposed to chance. This is, I think, why so many old people go about things with such feverish haste. They have to finish what they are doing while the light of day is still there for them and while they still have the strength to go forward and to create. I do not think they are behaving very wisely. True wisdom consists in doing what we have to do calmly, without restlessness and excitement, and leaving to God the cares of tomorrow that we cannot deal with today. Let us, then, continue on our pilgrimage, putting one foot in front of the other, until we reach the last inn—the inn of death, which is also a chapel.

The end of a pilgrimage is not a decline. It is an arrival. It is not a failure, but a success. Old age may look from the outside like a descent or even like a great fall. There is a way of speaking about old age that hints at this: declining years. I remember pictures showing life as a double staircase, ascending to the age of forty and then descending to death. This is true, of course, if you are only concerned with appearances, but if you go beyond them and penetrate to the heart of old age, it can be seen as the summit of a continuous ascent. Our pilgrimage brings us to a holy place at the top of a hill, the mountain of God. A few more steps and we are there!

When we reach the summit, we shall turn and look back at our past. The whole of our journey will be unfolded in front of us, there below, from the cradle to the grave. And from our mouths will come a great hymn of praise to God, a thanksgiving like that sung by the aged Simeon in the Temple. Standing in the last rays of the evening sun as they fall from the summit onto the plain below, we shall understand the meaning of our life as pilgrims and know that everything in it has been God's gift of love, even the sufferings that we have experienced in soul and body and even our humiliations and failures. We shall understand that God has led us to this height at the end. Then we shall turn again and, without any fear of the night that is about to fall, we shall enter it boldly in the confident hope that it is the prelude to a new sun.

Old age is going up. It is hard at times, but it is still an ascent. Who was it who thought of naming a Christian movement for old people in France "Life Ascending"? Whoever it was had the right idea.

My brothers, let us continue to climb as long as the evening sun is shining. We can always stop from time to time, get our breath back, and rest our tired old legs. But God is calling us from the heights and will not let us sit down for long. And he certainly will not let us go down again!

The pilgrimage is not over yet—let us be on our way! In front of us there is Christ himself, carrying his cross and showing us the way. And at the very top the Easter light of the Resurrection is shining.

Let us go up, brothers, in the evening sun.